# MUSTANG

## A New Breed of Pony Car 2005

**MATT DeLORENZO**

**MOTORBOOKS**
INTERNATIONAL

**On the front cover:** The 2005 Mustang balances retro
styling with the taut and precise surfaces demanded by
today's car buyers.

**On the frontispiece:** Even the lettering on minor details,
such as the GT badge, helps recall the Mustang's glory days.

**On the title page:** The Mustang GT boasts a powerful
300-horsepower V-8, complemented by large driving lights,
wide rocker panels, and 17-inch wheels.

**On the endpapers:** Design sketches of the 2005 Mustang.

**On the back cover:** The Mustang GT-R sits low to the
ground, hunkered down over 20-inch Pirelli racing slicks.
The GT can be specified with seats that contrast with the
interior, like these red buckets or black seats with red inserts.
The aluminum fascia dominates the dash, while the steering
wheel has a retro three-spoke look.

**Photos:** Ford Motor Company

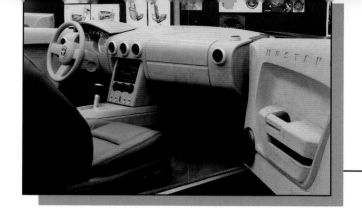

# Contents

# Dedication

To Jane—for 25 years and to 25 more.

# Acknowledgments

THIS BOOK IS THE CULMINATION OF THE EFFORTS OF many people, principally those who work behind the scenes at Ford Motor Co. to design, engineer, build, and market fabulous cars like the Mustang.

Many thanks go to Wes Sherwood of the public affairs department, who arranged interviews, chased down photos, and answered such esoteric questions as the meaning of the word hypereutectic. Also giving big assists were Sonia Mishra, John Arnone, Miles Johnson, Ray Day, Dan Bedore, Jim Cain, Said Deep, Afaf Farah, Jennifer Flake, and Anne Marie Gattari, who arranged my factory visits and is a terrific neighbor.

I'm always grateful to my boss, Thos Bryant, editor-in-chief of *Road & Track*, who allows me to moonlight from my day job as Detroit editor to tackle exciting projects like this book. I'd also like to thank freelance photographer Jim Fets, who was available in a pinch to help out with some of the great pictures that grace these pages.

More than thanks, I have tremendous admiration for the people at Ford, especially those who work on Team Mustang and SVT for their dedication and professionalism in building truly a world-class product. From the very top of the organization down to the line workers at the Dearborn Assembly plant that built the Mustang for 40 years and the workers now on the line at AutoAlliance International, the 2005 model is evidence of a job well done.

Last, but never least, thanks to my family, my wife Jane, who edits all my work, and our children, Amy and Stephen, who understand why the light burns late in our upstairs office.

# One

# A Legend Reborn

## The Philosophy Behind the New Pony Car

"When you're designing a new Mustang, you're the steward of 40 years of automotive history. If you don't get it right, you've got 8 million Mustang fans to answer to."

*—J Mays, Ford group vice president of design*

*How do you re-define a classic? Ford struggled intensely with that question before deciding that Mustang's heritage was too strong to ignore.*

HOW DO YOU REINVENT AN ICON? FOR 40 YEARS, one car—the Ford Mustang—defined an entire category of vehicles known as the pony car. And after 40 years, this archetype of the genre is the only one left, since General Motors stopped production of the Chevrolet Camaro and Pontiac Firebird in 2003.

While the Mustang underwent numerous transformations over those four decades, the basic architecture underpinning the 2004 model dates back to 1979 with the introduction of the Fox platform. This basic structure was in place for nearly two-thirds of the lifespan of the Mustang itself.

It was time for a change.

But what kind of change? Should the Mustang continue to evolve, making a great leap forward in design? Such a move could alienate the legions of traditionalists to whom the only real Mustangs are those from the 1960s. Should the car be a faithful reissue of the original, much like the Ford GT echoes the original GT40? Would such a move, while pleasing traditionalists, turn off a young generation of buyers who are more interested in high-horsepower front- and all-wheel-drive cars from Asia and Europe?

Adding to the design challenge were Ford's financial constraints. Given limited resources, a solid business case—and not sentiment—would be the bottom line in the decision of whether or not there would even be a new Mustang. The chance to come up with a new Mustang would be a once-in-a-career opportunity for those on the team, but a little voice in the background most certainly would whisper, "Don't mess it up."

The Mustang has seared itself into the country's collective consciousness. While many iterations of the Mustang have existed over the years, with all sorts of

*Signature cues, such as three-element taillights, play a major role in communicating that the 2005 Mustang is the genuine article.*

engines under the hood—inline fours and sixes, V-6s, turbo fours, V-8s and supercharged V-8s—the public has a pretty good idea of what a Mustang is and isn't. They couldn't necessarily tell you what it should be if you stood there with a blank sheet of paper in hand. But once they see the car in the flesh, they know whether it is or isn't a Mustang. That vague certainty made designing a new generation Mustang both difficult and risky.

J Mays, Ford group vice president of design, knows the risks. "When you're designing a new Mustang, you're the steward of 40 years of automotive history," he observes. "If you don't get it right, you've got 8 million Mustang fans to answer to."

So then, it was perfectly understandable that Ford, in looking to sustain America's love affair with the Mustang, went back to its stylistic roots—a long hood, short rear

*Mustang created a sensation with the public and the press at its 1964 launch during the New York World's Fair.*

deck. Not only is the profile familiar to all who sketched Mustangs on their high school notebooks, but so is the detailing, from the grille-mounted fog lamps to the three-bar taillights.

"By melding the true character of Mustang into these fully modern offerings, we've ensured that even the uninitiated will instantly recognize these cars as Mustangs," says Mays. "We went beyond their exterior designs to truly understand the extent to which Mustang has embedded itself in American culture."

Wrapping it in a new and yet familiar skin was a calculated move to ensure that buyers instantly understand what this car is all about.

The final design of the new Mustang is more faithful to the original car to make it seem as if that car had directly evolved to the 2005 model. Looking at both cars, it seems as if the 1970s Mustang II, which was based on the subcompact Pinto, never existed.

"We've made some mistakes with Mustang—the Mustang II is the most notable example," Mays admits. "If you dissect cues that people associate with Mustang, most people gravitate to the '64 1/2 to the '70 models. Those vehicles are lodged in people's minds as iconic Mustangs. We wanted to take those cues, and what we fill in between them becomes the modern part."

The iconic nature of the original is the reason the 2005 hews so closely to lines laid down 40 years ago. "Sometimes you try too hard to be new and you forsake 40 years of heritage," Mays explains. "The idea here is to re-create and get the lineage back on track. Once the lineage is reestablished in the production car, we can move forward again."

## BACK TO THE FUTURE

If someone were to awake from a Rip Van Winkle nap that started in 1968, they'd conclude that the more things change, the more they stay the same. As familiar as it looks and sounds with such features as V-8 power and a solid rear axle, the Mustang masks how much it has really changed. These changes are integral to the car's survival.

The fact that the Mustang still exists is a testament to the ingenuity of the product planners, designers, and

engineers at Ford. The key to the Mustang's success is that Ford has remained true to the basic Mustang concept in its approach to designing, engineering, and building the car. The Mustang isn't a sports car, but rather a four-place sporty coupe. It isn't high-tech for the sake of high-tech, but rather a state-of-the-art compilation of off-the-shelf technologies. It isn't exotic, it's appealing. Above all, it is accessible, offering tremendous bang for the buck when it comes to performance.

Ford didn't seek to create a new segment with the Mustang; the company was intent on offering an alternative to the popular, small sporty cars from Europe in the early 1960s. Chevrolet's answer was the rear-engine Corvair. In 1962, Ford mulled the idea of selling the Cardinal, a front-drive compact developed in Germany and sold in Europe as the Taunus. But the idea was scotched by then–general manager Lee Iacocca.

Iacocca, who later proved pivotal in selling the idea of the Mustang to Henry Ford II, said of the Cardinal in *Iacocca: An Autobiography*: "It was a fine car for the European market with its V-4 engine and front-wheel drive. But in the United States, there was no way it could have sold the 300,000 units we were counting on. Among other problems, it was too small and had no trunk." He told Henry Ford II, "We simply can't afford a new model that won't appeal to young buyers."

*An optional 289-ci V-8 was the first step towards transforming the Mustang from a mild-mannered pony car into a muscle car.*

*The original Mustang, pictured here in convertible trim, was hardly a road-burner with its base inline six. The car was more about style in an economical package.*

Instead, Donald Frey and program manager Hal Sperlich (who later created the minivan at Chrysler) tried another approach. It would be a sporty car based off the compact Falcon's rear-drive unit body. Iacocca pushed for the $75 million investment from a skeptical Henry Ford II. Like the Falcon, a 170-ci 101-horsepower inline six initially powered the Mustang, while a 260-ci 164-horsepower V-8 was optional. Later, the engine was upgraded to a 200-ci inline six rated at 120 horsepower and an optional 289-ci V-8 with output ranging from 200 to 271 horsepower. Offered in notchback and convertible body styles, the Mustang was an instant hit when it debuted on April 17, 1964. Priced at $2,368, the car sold 1 million units in its first two years, which Ford says is the only time a new car has ever reached that milestone in so short a time period.

*Much of the inspiration for the 2005 Mustang's body shape came from the 1965 Shelby GT350 2+2 fastback and the 1967–1968 Mustang.*

*Another car from the 1960s that had a huge impact on Mustang's popularity was the Highland Green GT used by Steve McQueen in the movie Bullitt. Note that the hood vents re-appeared on '05 Mustang concepts.*

Even in six-cylinder guise, the long hood and short deck proportions coupled with standard features like bucket seats and a floor-mounted shifter gave the Mustang a sporty flair that other economy cars lacked. That sporty image was further burnished with the introduction of the fastback 2+2 for 1965.

Ford had stolen a march on the competition—it was nearly two full model years before General Motors, Chrysler, and American Motors could bring competing pony cars to the market.

It is in the late 1960s when the facts about the Mustang and its stunning popularity begin to blur with the

*By 1971, the Mustang had grown from an economical pony car to a bulked-up muscle car that was as large as most intermediate cars of the era.*

*With notchback styling that suggested more of a personal luxury coupe than a high-performance sporting machine, the 1973 model remains the biggest and heaviest Mustang to date, flying in the face of the nameplate's heritage.*

myths of the Mustang, many of which are based on the public's perception of the car rather than actual success in the marketplace.

Many of these myths began to take shape with the 1967–68 models. Design changes further refined the car to a full fastback and the pony car image was pumped up into a muscle car persona with the infusion of serious performance. Larger and more powerful V-8s were wedged under the hood, a trend reflected by new labels such as Boss 302, Shelby 350, and Mach I. Further immortalizing the Mustang as part of America's pop culture was its starring role in Steve McQueen's *Bullitt*. On the track, Mustang earned respect in the hyper-competitive SCCA Trans-Am series, winning three

manufacturer titles. The Mustang continued to grow both figuratively and literally.

By 1971, the Mustang had changed from a lithe sporty compact to a 600-pound-heavier, 8-inch-longer muscle car fitted with big-block V-8 engines. Prices climbed to nearly double the introductory pricing and sales began to fall, plummeting below 150,000 units, thanks not only to higher pricing, but stiff competition from General Motors, Chrysler, and AMC.

But these are the models that pony car aficionados believe are the real Mustangs, though they never sold anywhere near the numbers of the less powerful and much simpler models that launched the series. According to the *Encyclopedia of American Cars*, by the early 1970s, Ford Vice President of Design Eugene Bordinat observed, "We started out with a secretary's car and ended up with a behemoth."

It wouldn't be the first nor last time that enthusiasts' desires were at odds with what the manufacturer was cooking up for the mass market. Many of these same enthusiasts will say the Mustang II wasn't a real Mustang. And while some point to the car as a reaction to the oil crisis and safety and emission concerns of the 1970s,

*Even before the first gas lines formed in 1973, Ford was working hard on a Mustang successor. This new-generation car, derived from subcompact car components was called Mustang II.*

*It wasn't long before enthusiasts clamored for V-8 power in the Mustang II, in addition to the base four and optional six-cylinder powerplants. The new model was called Mustang Cobra II.*

plans for the downsized Mustang II were well under way before the first gas line appeared.

## THE MUSTANG II SAGA

Hoping to turn around slumping sales, Ford returned to the original playbook for the Mustang, deriving an all-new model off the same component set used for the subcompact Pinto, albeit with a longer wheelbase and upgraded suspension and chassis bits. When the Mustang

II emerged as a '74 model, it was 20 inches shorter, 4 inches narrower, an inch lower, and nearly 500 pounds lighter than the car it replaced. Only two engines were offered: a 2.3-liter 88-horsepower four and a 2.8-liter 105-horsepower V-6. The V-8 didn't reappear until 1975.

The car was a disaster to the purists, but in its first year it sold over 385,000 units. Although the Mustang II hit that level only at the beginning of its five-year run, sales settled in at just under 200,000 units annually.

*The Cobra II evolved into the King Cobra by 1978 and was the last Mustang based on Pinto mechanicals.*

(in other words, really profitable) at levels that exceed 200,000 units. Smaller operations for high-priced specialty cars such as Corvette (of which about 30,000 are produced) can be made to work, although it should be noted that GM has added the Cadillac XLR at the Corvette Bowling Green assembly plant in Kentucky to help spread out costs.

It's that area between 50,000 and 200,000 units annually, especially for a vehicle with its own assembly plant, where the business case gets shaky. Although originally built in three assembly plants, by the 1970s Mustang production was scaled back to just one plant, in Ford's hometown of Dearborn, Michigan. From then on the Mustang operated in this no man's land, where just a few thousand units could mean the difference between life and death. Ford's archrival Chevrolet Camaro and Pontiac Firebird (which also reduced the number of factories building those two models from three to one remaining plant) had combined sales that in later years fell short of the Mustang's. The GM products averaged between 75,000 and 150,000 units annually. Eventually, GM recognized that it was a losing proposition and closed the St. Therese, Quebec, plant in 2003, ending a 36-year run for the General's pony cars.

There's no doubt that the auto business is all about the product, and at large manufacturers like Ford volume determines whether or not the lights are kept on at an assembly plant. Just like in the wild, survival is based on the concept of safety in numbers. In Detroit, that has meant big numbers. Although the Mustang has a tradition of using components from the Ford parts bin, it is unique enough to have its own assembly plant. As a rule, most plants operated by the Big Three are economically viable

**Above and right:** *Early chassis development of the 2005 Mustang involved Lincoln LS mules, giving rise to the speculation that the car would be based entirely on the DEW98 platform, underpinning the Lincoln and the Ford Thunderbird.*

The game had changed in many ways. Originally, pony cars were sporty compact cars for the masses. Eventually, they transformed into performance cars for enthusiasts whose viability depended on the ability to sell enough six-cylinder models (so-called secretaries' cars) to make the business case work. Often, many of these cars found their ways into low-margin rental fleets, which not only put additional pressure on profitability for the manufacturer, but also tended to depress resale values.

These changes worked in favor of the enthusiasts, a more vocal set than those buying the base cars. Consequently, the purists were able to dictate to Ford what they wanted in a Mustang. The question was how to build the kind of car these buyers wanted at sustained volumes far lower than any of the domestic manufacturers were accustomed to operate.

The aging Dearborn assembly plant that had been the Mustang's home for 40 years (initially, Mustang was built at three plants in Michigan, California, and New Jersey) was closed, with the last Mustang rolling off that line on Monday, May 10, 2004. In its place, Ford built a new showcase factory that would make F-150

pickup trucks in an ergonomic and environmentally
friendly way.

Further complicating matters was the fact that the
Fox platform, derived from the Ford Fairmont back in 1979,
had evolved to where it was unique within the Ford
system (the rear-drive Fairmont ceased production in 1984).
The new Mustang should, if possible, use an existing
platform or at least be based on an architecture from
which other vehicles at some point could be derived.

## DO THE DEW?

Phil Martens, Ford group vice president of product
creation, says the decision to remain rear-drive limited the
search. "Our initial thoughts were to base the new
Mustang on the DEW98 platform, which is used in the
Lincoln LS," Martens recalls. That would mean moving the
Mustang to Ford's Wixom, Michigan, assembly plant,
where the LS as well as the Ford Thunderbird (another
DEW98 derivative) are built.

"We decided, though, that one of the ingredients to
the Mustang's success has been having a variety of
models, everything from basic V-6 models up to high-
performance models like the SVT Mustang Cobra. We

wanted to build on that legacy rather than reinvent it,"
Martens says. The DEW98, with its independent rear
suspension, was also more expensive and complex than
the current Fox architecture.

Because variety and affordability are the keys to
Mustang viability, Martens says, "We needed a lower cost
architecture than the LS as well as flexibility."

A new platform was needed—one that would use
some of the bits from the LS, such as the independent
front suspension, and a low cost, tried-and-true three-link
solid axle at the rear. While this new platform is unique to
Mustang, it offers Ford the tantalizing possibility of
spinning some new, midsize rear-drive cars off the
Mustang architecture. Instead of coming from some
existing car, the Mustang, in a reversal of roles, may
someday spawn a new-age Falcon or some other
midsize sedan.

Meanwhile, the suitable production site for this
all-new Mustang turned out to be a plant in Flat Rock,
Michigan, which is run by Automotive Alliance
International, a joint Mazda/Ford assembly operation.
The Mustang is manufactured on the same final assembly
line as the Mazda 6.

The irony is that this new home of America's quintessential rear-drive pony car is the former home of the Ford Probe, a front-drive sports coupe that was originally conceived to carry on the Mustang legacy. Fortunately for the traditionalists, the rear-drive Fox platform proved too popular to allow the Mustang to go quietly into that good night.

*The new 2005 Mustang is built alongside the Mazda 6 sedan at the AutoAlliance International assembly plant in Flat Rock, Michigan.*

# Two

# Lessons Learned

## Understanding the Fox Platform and the Identity of the Mustang

The plan was to introduce the new front-drive Mustang while keeping the rear-drive Mustang "Classic" in production for several years, gradually phasing it out over time.

*The 1979 Mustang, based on the Fox platform, was larger and had a decidedly European feel. Although it retained the long nose, short deck proportion of the original, the clean surfaces were influenced by both imports and the wind tunnel.*

THERE'S NO QUESTION THAT THE 2005 MUSTANG IS all-new, from the sheet metal to the chassis—the first clean-sheet approach to the car in 25 years. And yet, the car is truly a product borne of the lessons learned from the Fox platform that served the Mustang so well for those 25 years.

The evolution of the Fox, especially the last two facelifts in 1994 and 1999, served as the template for how the 2005 model would be conceived, engineered, designed, built, and marketed.

No one, especially the team that worked on the original Fox, could have imagined that their work would be instrumental in creating an all-new car 25 years later. The Fox platform, which spawned a new Mustang in 1979, was somewhat of an anachronism when it bowed.

The times were turbulent. The industry had gone through two energy crises and economic downturns. Japanese imports were making huge inroads on domestic car market share. Downsizing and front-wheel drive were the orders of the day as U.S. makers struggled to meet ever-tightening fuel economy and emissions standards.

Against this backdrop, the new 1979 Mustang was still rear-drive and larger than the Mustang II it replaced. Like the original Mustang 15 years earlier, it was again based off a compact car, a size class up from the Pinto underpinnings used on the Mustang II.

The donor was the Fairmont, spiritual successor to the Falcon. The Fairmont replaced the Maverick in 1978 with both two- and four-door sedans and a special coupe called the Futura. Mercury also sold a version of the car as the Zephyr. The Fairmont was based on what was known internally as the Fox platform, and it was ideally suited for the redesigned Mustang. It was larger in wheelbase, width, and overall length and yet had a curb weight 200 pounds less than the Mustang II.

*It didn't take long for American tastes to exert an influence on the re-designed Mustang. By 1983, the GT sported a hood scoop and wilder graphics to match the V-8 power beneath the hood.*

The styling was crisp and clean and reflected a European influence that Jack Telnack, Ford executive director of North American car and truck design, brought home after a stint on the other side of the Atlantic Ocean. Offered in two-door notchback and hatchback versions, the Mustang had a tall greenhouse and a lean, drawn-out body that relied on lightweight steel, aluminum, and composites to keep the curb weight in check. The Mustang sported quad rectangular headlamps flanking an egg-crate grille. The look was modern and unique, unlike any Mustang before it, and yet with its long hood and short rear deck, it fit the classic pony car template.

The base engine of this new Fox-based Mustang was an inline 2.3-liter four rated at 88 horsepower, with a 140-horsepower turbocharged version of the same engine as

*The desire for European-inspired performance was strong in the Ford hierarchy, and in 1984, the Mustang SVO bowed with sportier handling, a turbocharged four that produced as much power as the V-8, and a unique biplane rear spoiler.*

*As front drive began sweeping the U.S. auto industry, Ford planned to use the technology in replacement for the rear-drive Mustang. The negative outcry was so great that the car was re-named Probe.*

**Above and opposite:**
*While Ford moved ahead with plans for the Probe, a study team worked on a rear-drive replacement code-named SN95, which would become the 1994 Mustang coupe and convertible, dropping the hatchback in the process.*

an option. A European-sourced 109-horsepower V-6 was also optional and when supplies ran short, a 91-horsepower inline six was offered. There was a 5.0-liter V-8 offered, but it only produced 140 horsepower. The revived Mustang was a hit, selling nearly 370,000 units in its first year. Both enthusiasts and the factory bean counters were happy with the car. The enthusiasts embraced both the Cobra Turbo and V-8 models, while the suits had a wide range of affordable models with economical four- and six-cylinder engines to help pump up the volume and meet federal fuel economy standards. By 1983 the car got a facelift and the first convertible version in a decade was added.

Although Ford returned to the basic formula that made the Mustang such a success in the first place, the gale force of change sweeping the industry would affect this icon. Change took two forms: The first was an attempt to Europeanize the look and performance of the top models; the second was a program to transform the Mustang altogether into a front-drive sporty coupe to meet the Japanese challenge.

While there's no doubt that the '79 model has clean European-inspired looks, the basic proportions of the car were still very American. With fake hood scoops and loud graphics, the Mustang couldn't be mistaken for anything coming from across the pond. By the mid-1980s,

however, Telnack, who rose to become vice president of Ford design, had revolutionized American styling with aerodynamic styling. The so-called jellybean cars featured soft, rounded contours and flush headlamps and glass. As part of this trend, the Mustang's corners were rounded off and flush headlamps were installed in a 1987 redesign.

On the engineering side, the influence of Ford's European operations was great as evidenced by the new flagship pony car, the 1984 SVO Mustang. SVO, which stood for Special Vehicle Operations, used turbocharging and intercooling to coax 175 horsepower from the car's 2.3-liter four-cylinder engine, later reaching the then magic number of 200 horsepower. The SVO boasted such

items as four-wheel disc brakes, low-profile 16-inch wheels and tires, a stiff suspension, and a controversial bi-plane rear spoiler. It also carried a premium of nearly $6,000 over the traditional GT, which offered the same levels of engine performance from its pushrod 5.0-liter V-8. Enthusiasts rejected the SVO version in favor of the GT's more traditional V-8 power and looks.

## FRONT-DRIVE SIREN SONG

While Ford worked to keep the Mustang contemporary by adopting the aero look, another program was under way to completely remake the car in the image of its Japanese competition. At the time, front-drive was considered the

*This early sketch of the SN95 was called Bruce Jenner for its trim, athletic shape that mirrored the looks of the famed Olympian. Clinics rejected the car for being too "pretty" to be a Mustang.*

silver bullet that would solve all the industry problems when it came to fuel economy standards and battling the increasing popularity of imports such as the Toyota Celica and Honda Prelude. Word that General Motors was working on front-drive replacements for the Chevy Camaro and Pontiac Firebird under the codename GM-80 undoubtedly further spurred Ford in this direction.

Since cars needed to be lighter and more fuel efficient, combining the engine and drivetrain at one end of the car would give maximum packaging efficiency.

While front-drive had the side benefit of offering better traction on slippery surfaces, it also limited the amount of horsepower that could be put down given the technology of the day. That meant no V-8s, but rather more fuel-efficient transversely mounted four- and six-cylinder powerplants.

Ford began work on a new program, codenamed SN8, to develop the front-drive successor to the Mustang. Along the way, Ford decided that it should turn to its new best friend, Mazda (in which it had a 25 percent stake), to help

*At the other end of the scale was the Rambo, a much more aggressive design with a pointy snout and huge scoops that wouldn't look unusual on a 2003 Pontiac Firebird. But, it was rejected for being too over-the-top.*

with this monumental transition from rear- to front-drive. Just as front-drive was the buzzword of the day, joint ventures with Japanese manufacturers had become *de rigueur*. GM and Toyota were building Corollas and Chevy Novas in California. Chrysler hooked up with Mitsubishi to share small-car technology. Ford and Mazda teamed up to build a new front-drive platform that would give Ford a new Mustang and Mazda the MX-6 coupe and 626 sedan from a plant in Flat Rock, Michigan. It also allowed the Japanese automaker to boost car sales at a time when exports to the United States were being restrained.

As a result of this cooperation, the program was renamed ST16, and the first design study of this front-drive Mustang was shipped to Mazda headquarters in Hiroshima for engineering studies. While development was under way, the car was redesigned again with a lower cowl and hood, a steeply raked windshield, and wraparound rear glass in an effort to make the car sportier and further differentiate it from the MX-6, even though the Ford was a hatchback and the Mazda wasn't.

Although the cars looked different, they shared the same platform and base 2.0-liter four-cylinder engine, while the Mustang GT model had a turbocharged four. Later, a 145-horsepower 3.0-liter Vulcan V-6 from the Taurus was introduced as an optional engine. The plan was to introduce the new front-drive Mustang while

keeping the rear-drive Mustang "Classic" in production for several years, gradually phasing it out over time.

When word leaked out of the new front-drive Mustang, enthusiasts rebelled and flooded Ford headquarters with phone calls and mail blasting the move. Rumors circulated that workers on the Flat Rock assembly line had actually pried Mustang badges off pilot production models. Such was the hue and cry over the naming issue that Ford decided to call the car Probe, a named used on a series of aerodynamic research and show cars that were built in the late 1970s and early 1980s.

The Mustang that wasn't a Mustang debuted at the Chicago Auto Show in 1988. Ford was about to conduct a grand experiment in whether a new front-drive pony car built with a Japanese partner could knock off the rear-drive Mustang, which for all its shortcomings still retained a loyal core of followers.

While the Probe had the advantages of an all-new design, good quality, and the then-perceived technical superiority of front-wheel drive, the Mustang still offered by Ford was hardly a pushover. It was affordable, offering a choice of economical four-cylinder power (the V-6 was dropped in 1986) or a V-8 in coupe, hatchback, or convertible body styles.

Launched in March 1988, the Probe sold 133,650 in its first complete model year (1989) compared to 161,148

*The compromise look for the SN95 was called the Schwarzenegger concept, which toned down the brutal muscularity of the Rambo and yet had more bulk than the svelte Jenner.*

Mustangs. Both cars, however, were on a downward slide with Mustang bottoming out at 80,247 sales in 1991, a year in which Probe came closest to matching Mustang sales by moving 76,295 units. The next year, Probe dropped to 63,659 units, while Mustang rallied somewhat to 86,036.

A redesigned Probe was introduced for the 1993 model year, gaining 2 inches in overall length and employing a new Mazda 2.0-liter four-cylinder engine for the base model and a Mazda-built 164-horsepower 2.5-liter V-6 for the GT. Sales bounced back to 90,435 units, but began to slide again. Even with the upgrades, the second-generation Probe's sales all but collapsed and the

car was axed after the 1998 model year. The third-generation Probe, which was to be based off the midsize Ford Contour/Mercury Mystique platform, bowed in 1999 as a Mercury Cougar instead.

## RECRAFTING THE FOX

The soft demand convinced Ford management that perhaps there was still some life in the rear-drive Mustang concept and authorized a study team to develop a major rework of the car on the Fox platform. The Mustang had not only bested its in-house rival, it survived in what was still a fiercely competitive segment. Ford was correct to rethink its approach. There evidently existed a market for

a traditional rear-drive American pony car, although keeping the volumes above 100,000 units was crucial to long-term viability. The study team's mission was clear: to develop plans that would enable the Mustang to continue on the Fox platform and yet address the many shortcomings of its aging component set.

Ford decided to use the new Mustang program to test the company's new World Class Timing (WCT) car development process, which was designed to reduce costs and bring cars to market in record time. There would be a new Mustang if, and it was a big if, strict cost guidelines and timetables were met. The goals were set high: 20 percent of the development costs had to be

slashed while taking a quarter of the time out of the development process. In other words, the Mustang would come to market in three years instead of the traditional four, and the team would have to do it on a budget of $700 million at a time when the average new car program cost $1 billion.

The program, dubbed SN95, began with a series of focus groups and design studies that went to clinics in an effort to find the right look for the redesign.

Bud Magaldi, the design manager who worked on SN95, said there were three approaches to the redesign. "One early idea we had for the 1994 model had a very nice, modern look," he says. "But its overall shapes were

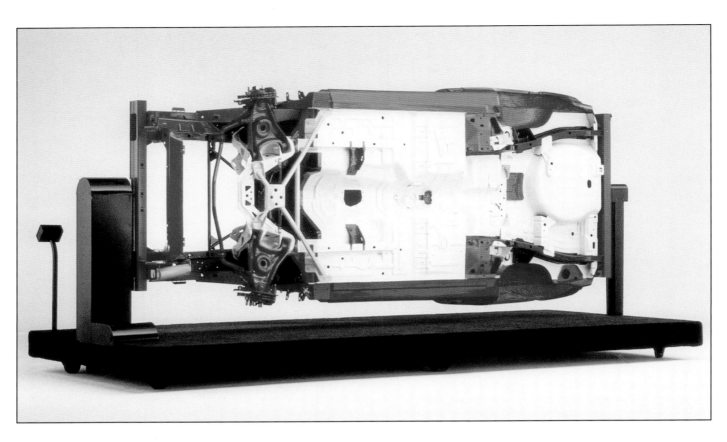

Opposite and left: *While the basic Fox floor pan was retained, these stampings, shown in white, are just part of the many changes that were made to the Mustang. The other body panels and braces, shown in red and yellow, were new. These extensive changes led to the re-classification of the platform as the Fox-4.*

too smooth, too clean and friendly, too nice. It was just a little bit too sweet, too smooth for the real Mustang lovers. Our research clinics proved to us that a car could be perceived as too European or Japanese."

That car was known as "Bruce Jenner" for its lean, athletic look with rounded corners. The second proposal, way over on the other end of the scale, was nicknamed "Rambo" for its sharply chiseled lines, aggressive nose, and large scoops. "It was a Batmobile-type thing," Magaldi said at the time. "It was a very aggressive car that was gutsy and dramatic, like a Stealth bomber."

The third concept, in between, was known as "Arnold Schwarzenegger," a design that had the same athletic look as the Jenner concept, but with more muscle and bulk. Those who liked the Ford Probe also liked the Jenner version, and it was concluded that the look wasn't true to the Mustang heritage. The Rambo was considered too over-the-top. "The focus groups kept saying, 'The car in the middle is the one we want,'" Magaldi says. "It had the

scoops; it looked like the Mustang, even with the horse emblems off. Our goal was to bring back the Mustang heritage in a very contemporary way. That was the key and that seemed to be what people wanted us to do."

The one theme that kept coming back to the team over and over again was that the Mustang had to look American. With its long hood, short rear deck, and especially the detailing, the design team captured the essence of the original Mustang, but in a very contemporary way. Part of that modern feel was also due to the car's detailing. "We kept the design simple," Magaldi says. "We avoided hang-on stuff. We didn't use any tape or decals. All of our graphics—the horses, the bars, the GT symbol—are all three-dimensional."

That combination of detailing taken from the original Mustang and executed in a contemporary fashion was also used on the interior. "By having a rich history, the Mustang provided us with dozens of styling accents from the past that we could draw on and enhance," says

*In 1999, the Mustang was re-designed on the Fox-4 platform to carry more overt references to the original Mustang. Among these changes were sharper character lines running fore to aft and large, non-functional hood and side scoops.*

*The retro-inspired look of the '99 Mustang was carried through to the 2004 40th Anniversary Mustang pictured here.*

Emiline King, interior designer of the SN95. "We wanted to give drivers and passengers a taste of the earlier models in a modern way."

The biggest similarity was the return of the dual cockpit interior, which featured a two-tone dash treatment with a dark upper and a lighter lower. That two-tone approach was carried over onto the GT's bucket seats, which had contrasting inserts just like the original Mustang.

Under the hood, the SN95 received its most significant upgrade by losing the base four-cylinder powerplant in favor of a 3.8-liter OHV V-6 rated at 145 horsepower. Meanwhile, the pushrod 5.0-liter V-8 returned, producing 215 horsepower and 285 ft-lb of torque. Later in the 1994 calendar year, the SVT Mustang Cobra was introduced using a 240-horsepower version of that engine.

With limited resources and the mandate to use the existing architecture, the SN95 team still managed significant upgrades to the chassis and body structure. "We really emphasized body rigidity," says Will Boddie, then director of small and midsize cars at Ford. Of the car's 1,850 parts, 1,330 of them were new or improved. That solid foundation was the key to tuning the chassis to deliver improved ride and handling. So many changes were made under the skin that the company began referring to the platform as Fox-4 (the 4 referring to the 1994 model year) to reflect the upgrades.

Part of this change and the quest for a stiffer body meant dropping the hatchback and concentrating only on a coupe and convertible. The coupe featured a sharply raked backlight that paid homage to the Mustang's original fastback design. The Fox-4 resulted in a car that had a

*Recognizing that limited-production-run Mustangs have always been a hit, Ford decided to do a special edition of the 2001 model trading on the popularity of Steve McQueen's Mustang GT in the 1968 movie Bullitt. Only 6,500 Bullitt GTs were built. These cars sported classic five-spoke alloy wheels, an aluminum shifter, and were offered in only three colors—black, dark blue, and Highland Green.*

longer wheelbase, a wider track, revised front suspension geometry, and across-the-board use of four-wheel disc brakes. The rear suspension remained a live axle located by four trailing links, and base models were fitted with a rear roll bar for the first time. GT models benefited from the use of four shocks, two mounted vertically and two horizontally to control axle windup during hard acceleration and braking. The car was a success, selling nearly 160,000 units in the 1994 model year.

The team delivered its product in 35 months, thanks in part to cutting the number of engineering prototypes needed from three to two, cutting five months from the normal 30 months needed for tooling time on major body panels. Above all, by co-locating all major disciplines in one place, from design and engineering to marketing and manufacturing, Ford established a streamlined methodology for developing new products quickly. The team concept developed for SN95 is still in use today on the 2005 model.

If the 1994 redesign of the Mustang established the processes that would be used to develop future models, the 1999 redesign developed the templates for design and marketing, and established further flexibility in the

mechanical package to ensure the volumes needed to keep the car in production.

This time, design took another step in grafting more overt classic Mustang cues on the car. The front end was revised with a larger intake. The chrome pony was surrounded by a new chrome corral, and a nonfunctional

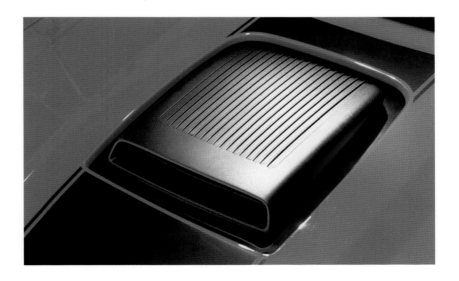

*The success of the Bullitt GT led to the development of the Mach 1, a modern interpretation of that legendary muscle car. The most prominent cues lifted from the earlier model were the black hood treatment and shaker hood scoop.*

scoop dominated the hood. The side scoops were made larger, and sharper character lines defined the scalloped sides, while the rear highlighted the three vertical bar taillight theme that was so popular on the original Mustang. The softer contours all around the car were given more edge and the car's overall look made more muscular by sharply drawn fender flares.

While the hard points of the Mustang remained the same, the V-6 engine benefited from a revised intake manifold, new heads, freer flowing exhaust, and horsepower increased from 150 to 190 horsepower. The 4.6-liter SOHC V-8, which replaced the pushrod 5.0-liter powerplant in 1996, saw a gain in power from 225 to 250 horsepower. Traction control was offered for the first time on the '99 model and, in keeping with the Mustang's image, was tuned to allow some straight-line wheel slip (read burnouts).

Other upgrades included revised spring rates (variable coils were replaced by linear-rated 450-pound coil springs), and underbody bits such as frame rails were fully boxed to further stiffen the chassis. For the first time,

*Workers gather around the final Mustang to roll off the line at the Dearborn Assembly Plant on May 10, 2004, ending a 40-year run at the facility.*

Mustang came with a choice of rear suspensions. The V-6 and GT models retained their solid axle setups while the SVT Cobra was launched later in the 1999 calendar year with an independent rear. Slick engineering allowed the modular built-up independent rear to be bolted into the same space as the solid axle on the same assembly line as the V-6 and GT models.

The SVT Cobra promised 320 horsepower to rival the output of the Chevy Camaro SS and Pontiac Firebird Trans Am. However, owners noticed that the cars didn't seem as robust as the specs indicated. Subsequent tests revealed that the cars were 25 to 50 horsepower short due to faulty intake components. Ford ceased production of the Cobra during the 2000 model year while it fixed the problem.

## NO. 1 WITH A BULLITT

Still, the retro styling theme of the Mustang clicked with enthusiasts. Further playing to the nostalgia factor was a series of special one-off models based on the GT. The first was the Bullitt GT, a 6,500-unit run, designed to pay homage to the '68 Mustang used by Steve McQueen in the detective thriller *Bullitt*. Painted the same Dark Highland Park green as the movie car (or blue or black if the buyer preferred), the Bullitt GT sported five-spoke aluminum alloy wheels, an aluminum fuel filler door, a large hood scoop, and chromed exhaust tips. Inside were an aluminum shifter, aluminum pedals, and a stitch pattern to the bucket seats that recalled 1960s Mustangs. Although the Bullitt offered only 10 horsepower more than the stock GT, improvements to the exhaust system, throttle body, and intake manifold widened the torque band considerably and helped give the car a burbling exhaust note. The suspension was tauter and the ride height lowered. The cumulative effect of these subtle changes gave this particular special-edition Mustang a character all its own that fit neatly from a performance standpoint and a sticker price between the stock GT and the SVT Cobra.

SVT Cobra went away for the 2002 model year and returned in 2003 with an Eaton supercharger that boosted output up to 390 horsepower. This not only pushed up the performance quotient considerably for the more

expensive SVT model, but it also widened the gap back to the stock GT. Ford came back with another special-edition model in 2003, the Mach 1, which again played to the car's nostalgia. Equipped with a shaker matte black two-tone hood, the Mach 1 had special five-spoke alloy wheels and the Bullitt's aluminum shifter, pedals, and fuel filler door. Under the hood, however, was the previous SVT Cobra's 4.6-liter DOHC V-8 with 320 horsepower. Like the Bullitt GT, the Mach 1 was intended to be a limited-run, one-year-only model, but it proved so popular that Ford brought it back for the 2004 model year. The 2005 Mustang will debut only as a coupe, followed by a

convertible, but Ford has made it clear that the SVT Cobra will be back and special-edition models like the Bullitt and Mach 1 will reappear from time to time as need dictates.

Although the styling of the 2005 Mustang overtly pays homage to the 1967–70 models, its real substance, from the hardware to how and why things are done, has grown out of the two cars based on the SN95. It's this building block approach that not only keeps the original rear-drive pony car formula intact, but will also provide a familiar feel to the car's performance. The melding of the original design with the latest in performance has the makings of an instant classic.

*The Mach 1 was produced during the 2003–2004 model years. Its success almost guarantees its re-appearance on the next generation car.*

# Three

# Familiar by Design

## Developing the Mustang's Retro Look

"This car is designed to be an American classic.
This is the only one left."

—J Mays, Ford group vice president of design

**The biggest challenge facing Ford designers was finding a shape that paid homage to Mustang's roots and at the same time presented a fresh face. The 2005 Mustang balances retro styling with the taut and precise surfaces demanded by discriminating consumers.**

WHAT IS IT THAT MAKES A MUSTANG A Mustang? With that simple question, the designers began their search for the shape that would define this American icon not only for traditional Mustang enthusiasts, but also for a whole new generation of buyers unaware of the car's origins.

For J Mays it was a daunting challenge to do the right car for Ford, while at the same time enduring the criticism that as a designer he is a one-trick pony, that trick being retro design. Mays earned his reputation at Volkswagen and Audi where he was involved with the new VW Beetle and the Audi TT. After he assumed the role of design vice president at Ford in 1998, Mays delivered the retro-inspired Thunderbird (though this project predated his employment), followed by such nostalgic show cars as the Ford Forty Nine and 427 and the 2005 Ford GT, virtually a reissue of the original GT40.

When the wraps came off the Ford Mustang GT concept at the 2003 North American International Auto Show, some critics said Mays was incapable of doing an

*Designers drew their inspiration for the '05 model's driving lights from a number of vintage Mustangs. They range from the small fog lamps used on '65–'66 models to much larger lights on the '69 Mach 1 and Boss Mustangs.*

all-new car. Mays rejected this view out of hand, believing that the familiar shape of the Mustang was crucial to the car's success.

"We have gotten to the point where we are just so enamored with the next new thing that we have forgotten that we have this fantastic history," Mays says. "I've been

fairly or unfairly criticized as looking over my shoulder too much. But a modern car is essentially a product stripped of its history in my viewpoint. I may be at risk of being thrashed and hung up by my toes, but I refuse to go down this elitist designer path where everyone says you have to create modern cars; it's a sin to look backward.

*The rear-end treatment of the 2005 Mustang faithfully re-creates the quarter window treatment, but it must rely on a black border in the rear glass to re-create the "U" shape in the backlight.*

Give me a break! We do 80 cars that are nothing but looking forward. If we want to have a look over our shoulder because there are 8 million customers who want it, that's our business."

But Mays also believes very strongly that retro styling cues are not the sole ends to justify the Mustang's existence. Rather, they are the means to attract buyers to what is essentially a modern automobile.

"The trick to all these cars that have a heritage to them is that you actually create two or three focal points and leave a lot of blank space in between," Mays says.

"Because if I took off some of the design cues of the Mustang, I would have a rather dramatic-looking coupe that no one would recognize. The whole idea is leaving the big blank spaces and having a couple of cues where people say, 'Oh yeah, I get it,' and let them fill in the blanks. This allows the car to resonate with people because it is filled with their own personal meaning."

Meanwhile, those blank spaces allow the modern aspects of the car to come through to those who have no preconceived notions of what Mustang is or should be. That way, Mays hopes to reach a new generation of buyers.

The rear end of this Shelby GT500 inspired a debate on whether or not the 2005 Mustang should have a ducktail spoiler built into the body.

Below: *It was decided that the Mustang shouldn't have a rear spoiler built into the bodywork, since it would blur the distinction between V-6 and GT models. As a result, the V-6 has a clean rear deck lid, while the GT has an add-on spoiler.*

"The idea of bringing the Mustang back and making it relevant to all us [older] guys, but also to our kids, is what's driving this design," Mays explains. "This car is designed to be an American classic. This is the only one left. Everything else has fallen by the wayside. I think there is honesty in this design that doesn't come through with the Thunderbird. That car has a very different and limited market. Once you've sold four years of Thunderbird at 25,000 [units] per year, nearly everyone who wanted one has got one. That car just doesn't have the following that Mustang has."

## A VISUAL HISTORY

Mays collaborated with designer Doug Gaffka to research early Mustangs for inspiration. "We laid out a visual photography audit that went from 1964 1/2 to 1970, picked up a little of the Euro-inspired Mustangs of 1979 and later, as well as the last two generation Mustangs. We grouped these into side profiles, front graphics, rear graphics, and details such as different front-end treatments, fog lamps, spoilers, scoops, nomenclature, different hoods, different stripes, and different graphic treatments. We also looked at different wheels, C-pillars, window graphics and, on the rear, different iterations of the three vertical taillamp theme that all Mustangs had up until today."

The visual audit was backed up by extensive conversation with people inside and outside the company, including Mustang club members. It soon became apparent that the "real" Mustang was the 1967–70 version.

"We knew we wanted to have a '67 Mustang in terms of spirit, but not a literal copy," Mays says. "We didn't want it to represent the pony cars from '64 1/2 to '66, but rather the muscle cars from '67 to '70."

Using all this assembled imagery as a guide, Mays and Gaffka focused in on one particular model—the Shelby GT350. "We knew that was the profile we wanted and that's where the little rear window in the C-pillar came from."

But first, the proportion of the car needed to be correct. All the graphic cues, such as the C-pillar windows

*In profile, the Mustang exhibits the classic long hood and short rear deck look that has defined the breed. Also of great importance was the relationship of the wheels to the body and the rocker extensions that give the GT some muscle.*

*The V-6 version of the Mustang has a more lithe body. By using black rocker extensions, the body appears to wrap beneath the car. In order to fill the wheel arches, taller profile tires are specified for the stock 16-inch wheels.*

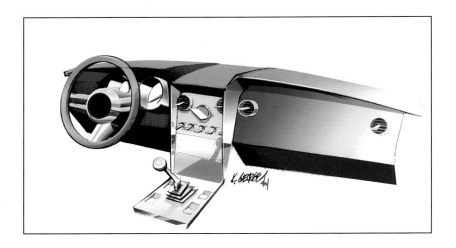

*From the beginning, as these early sketches indicate, the interior was designed to be clean, uncluttered, and technical in appearance.*

and scoops, wouldn't make any difference if the body beneath was not correct

Starting with the 2000 model, Mays and Gaffka moved the front wheels forward an inch and a half to emphasize the long hood and short rear deck proportion of the original. "Moving the wheels ahead gave us a great dash-to-axle ratio (the distance between the trailing edge of the front wheels and the leading edge of the door), but we wanted to emphasize the long hood even more than any car that is out on the road today," Mays explains.

That led to pushing the front edge of the hood out over the grille, which adversely affects aerodynamics but gives the Mustang a distinctive shark-nose look similar to the '67 model. "By not having an aero nose on it, but by putting a shark-nose on it, we added about four inches of length to the nose visually," Mays says. "That sort of long hood, close-coupled teardrop greenhouse, and short rear deck became the proportion we were chasing."

Beyond the long hood/short deck profile of the car, Mays also was concerned about the car's stance. He wanted a wide, muscular look for the car, a look that meant business. "Our research studies have shown that both the F-150 pickup and the Mustang are considered tough. Not only does the car look tough, people who own them feel tough. What I wanted to do was to create this incredible stance—I wanted a big tough shoulder on the car," Mays adds. "That became the driving factor—getting the stance and the shoulder right."

That shoulder resulted in a strong, unbroken character line that runs from the car's nose to tail, accentuated by large wheel flares to pump up the car's muscular look. Much time was also spent working on the wheel-to-body relationship. In fact, the V-6 model was fitted with smaller 16-inch wheels and taller profile tires were specified in order to fill up the wheelwells.

"Doug and I spent a lot of time on that wheel-to-body relationship, the proportion as well as the cross-section and profile of the car. Other concerns were front and rear overhang and where the cabin was going to sit," Mays recalls. "Putting all this retro stuff aside, this is what the car was really all about—how to create a correct proportion for the car, finding the proper length for the hood, the proper teardrop cabin, the short rear deck, the proper stance and cross-section. Only then did we start looking at a modern way to incorporate some of the features from the original cars on it."

At this point in the project, Gaffka handed the design team over to Larry Erickson, a former GM designer and creator of ZZ Top's Cadzilla hot rod.

"Mustang's success was that it was classically different from other cars," Erickson says. "Take the GTO for instance. The GTO was about taking a Tempest and stuffing a large motor in it. If you didn't have the motor you didn't have a GTO. With the Mustang, even if you had a six instead of a V-8, you still had the Mustang. It had a clear proportion and clean look. That was the driving force when we did the new car."

## FINESSING THE FASCIAS

That's not to say that the new design sprang forth complete from the drawing board. There was painstaking work, much of it in the clay model stage to finesse not only the proportion, but also the detailing.

"You can see in the natural progression of the clay models where the new Mustang evolved from the SN95," Erickson explains. "In the early models, you can see a lot of the old Mustang in the way the surfaces open and close, and the greenhouse has a swooping arch."

Slowly, as the proportion of the car began to shift, graphic details of early Mustangs were baked into the design. "From the very beginning we decided we were going to the three-segment taillamp and we were going to a grille with the headlamps outboard of that."

While some details such as headlamp placement and the taillight graphics were a given, other details such as the large grille-mounted fog lamps for the GT were open to great debate.

"Over time, the driving lamps were in and out, then in again, then out again. They got smaller and then larger," Erickson laughs. "Finally, we decided on the really large ones because we wanted the GT to be instantly recognizable from the V-6 model."

Mays concurs. "We wanted those powerful, far-and-away oversized fog lamps in the grille to be flamethrowers. I think, to be honest, we were a little influenced by the Subaru WRX. There was no rhyme or reason why they needed to be that large, but we wanted to be extra aggressive."

That aggressiveness extended to other areas of the GT, including the sill extensions on the rocker panels and larger air inlets below the bumper line. The GT is also equipped with beefy five-spoke alloy wheels fitted with low-profile tires. The V-6, on the other hand, has a much leaner look, with a small lower snorkel and sills that wrap beneath the body. Optional 10-spoke alloy wheels are equipped with fake knock-off hubs. "From a design

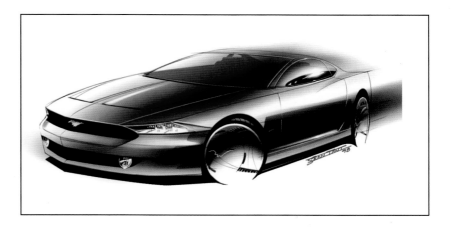

*Early design sketches show a very modern interpretation of the Mustang concept.*

*These sketches show a retro flavor in the Mustang, a direction that was ultimately settled upon.*

perspective, I prefer the V-6 over the GT because it is more basic," Mays admits. "It doesn't rely on big chin spoilers; it's light underneath because of the way the sill wraps underneath, and the 16-inch wheels with the taller profile tires hold it up well, which is really unusual these days."

This model differentiation sparked debate over the rear-end treatment of the car. Originally, designers proposed a small ducktail spoiler as part of the rear fender and deck lid stampings for the car.

"There was a whole lot of conversation about the philosophy of the ducktail," Erickson says. "If we were only doing the GT, it probably would have had a ducktail on it. But in reality, we were working on a car that would

be the pony car V-6 and the more muscle-oriented V-8 GT. I know that overall we're getting away from the pony car concept with this design, but adding the ducktail puts it at odds with the V-6. It dramatically changes the signature of the car." Instead of the ducktail, the designers went with a clean deck lid and decided to use an add-on rear wing to distinguish the GT from the V-6.

There was also considerable debate over the rear-end treatment regarding the three-element taillamps. One proposal pushed by Mays had very short yet wide lamps positioned at the top of the opening that ran almost the complete width of the tail. "I really liked this rear end, but the team made me pull the lights all the way down. I was hell bent on those taillamps for six months, but they talked me out of them and I'm glad they did."

Before settling on the connected three-element lamps, Erickson says the team also experimented with having the individual elements separated by sheet metal, an idea eventually rejected due to cost. "Sure it would have been nice, but at what price? The money for such a small detail could be used elsewhere, say on different interior materials that have a greater impact on the customer," Erickson says.

And there was room for small details that only the hard-core Mustang enthusiast can appreciate, like the gills inside the headlamp bezels that mimic similar openings on the nose of early Mustangs. "Sometimes you have to have fun with things," Erickson says. "Sometimes we take things so seriously. Headlamps have gotten to the point where they are their own study in geometry inside the headlamp can. We wanted this element in the bezel to relate to the center grille." It's a detail that's hard to pick out because the bezels themselves are a black matte finish. "The gill is a connection to the original, but we didn't want it jumping out at you," Erickson explains.

One styling element Mays had hoped to incorporate into the car was the horseshoe-shaped backlight of the early Mustangs. But since the car would be offered as both a coupe and a convertible, more conventional rear glass with a straight edge was required so that the same rear deck could be used on both models. "You see that line is on the car in the black glazing of the glass, but it's

not the same," Mays says. "I would have loved to have that line on the car, and had we not had to build the convertible with the same rear quarter panel, we would have had it. It would have been a fantastic update."

Knowing when to stop with adding these heritage cues was equally important as knowing what details needed to be on the car to make it a Mustang. "There was debate on whether or not we put the corral around the pony, and so on. You could start throwing everything at it because you're having so much fun with the details. But there is a point where you have loaded up with too much. It's like too many notes in a piece of music," Erickson says.

The same goes for the contours of the body. Originally, the side featured a character line that formed a "C" in the side of the car as well as various proposals for a

*An interior buck shows a slightly different approach with such features as a dash-mounted analog clock and individual gauges for fuel and water temperature.*

*As the design continued to evolve, two themes emerged—the shark-like nose and the three-element taillamps. This clay still retains the SN95 greenhouse but incorporates such cues as the auxiliary driving lights used on the GT.*

side scoop. "Because of the strong character line running fore to aft, it seemed more natural to turn the line up and end it for a hockey stick look than turn it back forward for a side scallop," Erickson says, adding that for simplicity's sake, the team decided to dispense with a side scoop.

As Mays puts it, many of these details were like "putting a pastiche of crap on the car. Oh, by the way, a pastiche of crap will end up on the car because people are out there feverishly working away to come up with some ill-fitting scoop for the thing. But that's okay, let them have fun."

By minimizing the character lines, the Mustang has a clean, crisp, machined look that gives it a modern air. And unlike the original, where the rear end tended to fall away from the front, the new Mustang has a forward gesture to its stance.

In clinics, the design fared well among old and young alike, Erickson says. Older people immediately got the connection to the original, while young people had their own take on it. "One of our guys came back and said that he learned a new term, 'old school.' He thought at first that it was negative but came to realize that it's just an observation, and from there you decide whether you like it or not," Erickson says.

"There is a difference between classic cars, retro, and old school," Mays says. "I see the Mustang representing old school. It is the automotive equivalent of Abercrombie & Fitch. I think we ended up with a pretty pure statement and it's a statement we won't have to facelift. Over the six or seven years that this thing is in production, the only thing we have to do to it now is to create the different limited series that should come to the market and constantly excite people."

## THE INSIDE STORY

An eye-catching exterior alone isn't enough to guarantee success in a hyper-competitive market. Interiors are playing an increasingly important role of delivering on the promise of the car's overall design, and the Mustang is no exception.

"The interior has to offer some of the identity that comes with the past history of the cars," Erickson says,

*Early clay modeling shows some experimentation with bumper height and its relation to the large headlamps. The bumper line was eventually lowered to open up the front end of the car and eliminate the need to cut into the bumper fascia.*

but adds, "it also presented us with an opportunity to do something that was more modern at the same time."

Cost is also a serious consideration, and one of the keys to the Mustang's success is affordability. In order to

In the rear, designers experimented with the three-element taillamps individually set into the body. Again, note the SN95 C-pillar.

J Mays, group vice president of design, wanted this taillamp treatment for the Mustang, a look that was determined by the team to be too European or Japanese and was ultimately rejected.

This mockup displays another alternative front-end treatment for the Mustang. The split headlamp design was later adapted to the Mustang GT-R show car.

keep the base price of the V-6 model under $20,000, the Mustang team was under a lot of pressure to minimize costs.

"We got a hard, plastic interior," Mays says of the new Mustang. "That interior is less expensive than the outgoing interior, believe it or not. Yet we were able to create in that interior a couple of visual anchors that your eyes go to, and people say you've done a fantastic interior."

The most prominent visual anchor is an optional, ribbed aluminum insert that covers the length of the dash. "We made this real aluminum strip that runs across the instrument panel an option on every possible vehicle,

whether it is a V-6 or a GT," Mays says. He points out that the large chrome-ringed vents and gauge cluster add to this upscale aura. "This draws your eyes to several focal points in the interior, that, along with the steering wheel, take your eyes off the fact that you're sitting in a pretty bare-bones interior," Mays says.

And if the vents look familiar, that's no coincidence, according to Erickson. "This is the same design vent that we use on the F-150, although it has a slightly different adjustment. With any high-volume car, you will end up with the corporate center stack that includes the radio and

**Above and next page:**
*This early clay captures the flavor of vintage Mustangs and yet, the surfacing and detailing is contemporary.*

ventilation system. Adding the aluminum panel gives a big personality shift to the interior."

The interior design is an exercise in simplicity, says Mays. "It's the muscle car interior that you think you remember. It has this hard eyebrow, symmetrical with this little indentation in the middle, and a big, honking piece of ribbed aluminum under it and big chrome gauges. We played with the typeface on the gauges. We got these illegible, but really fun, very tall numbers on the gauges. The ergonomics people hate us, but the type looks really cool."

While it does have the flavor of an old muscle car, Erickson says that if you look at an interior from that era, the differences are stark. Most of those interiors had hard metal surfaces, where in their place on the new Mustang are grained plastic pieces. And while the seats sport the same sort of tuck-and-roll pattern of the 1960s, they're plusher and more supportive. In addition, color contrasting seat and door inserts help liven up the interior.

One area of considerable debate and ultimate change was the shifter. Originally envisioned as a round, chrome knob on a short shaft, the chromed plastic knob

*In addition to experimenting with alternative taillamp treatments, these clays also are used to test different wheel designs, such as the five-spoke (top) and the ten-spoke (above) alternatives.*

*Although it derives its inspiration from the 1968 Mustang, the new model has a much cleaner exterior and a forward gesture to its stance, while the older car looks as if the rear end is sagging.*

*The GT originally had smaller auxiliary lights, no headlamp covers, and additional intakes on the corners of the front fascia.*

tooled for production felt cheap. A new knob, with a combination black soft touch center and brushed aluminum outer has replaced it, although Mays favored the use of the solid aluminum knob found on Ford's European Puma sport coupe.

The steering wheel also has a retro, yet contemporary flavor to it, with its aluminum three-spoke design and padded center hub that contains an airbag. "That is the thing that we are always balancing," says Erickson, "contemporary, yet familiar. You could get it to look really different, but that different look could translate into a short shelf life. We biased ourselves toward doing the interior as modern as possible without setting it up to age quickly. We want to have a timeless design, much like some modern designs of the 1950s that still look contemporary today."

## FROM REALITY TO CONCEPT

Bucking the trend of unveiling a concept car and then working forward with the production version, the new Mustang was well under way when Mays commissioned two concept versions of the car. Richard Hutting, of the California Concept Center, which does advanced design work for Ford, built the concepts.

"The idea was to grease the skids and let the public know that a new Mustang was on the way," Mays says. He adds that the work was farmed out to California because "we were so tucked into the production car, we didn't want the design team to get

After the production car had been decided, Ford commissioned two show cars—a GT coupe and GT convertible—to introduce the new design to the public. Industry practice has been to first create a concept, test public reaction, and then establish the production version.

The Mustang GT convertible concept, like the coupe, sports a more aggressive front end than the final production version. Yet, like the 2005 Mustang, there's no mistaking its heritage.

*In profile, both the coupe and convertible have a beefier lower rocker and the hood is much flatter than the production GT and V-6 models, which have more crown for a slightly taller stance.*

excited about the concepts and take their eyes off the execution of the production car."

In addition to being used as communication and promotion tools for the upcoming Mustang, Mays saw the concepts as an opportunity to experiment with forms that could be used on future designs.

The show cars were shortened and lowered by 2 inches and presented as two-seaters. The convertible

The GT coupe concept has a scoop just ahead of the rear wheels. Designers decided that having one on the production model would give the 2005 Mustang a cluttered appearance. However, a covered C-pillar window treatment is a future possibility.

Ford designers also experimented with a glass roof on the GT coupe concept. Both show cars are two-seaters, and in the back of the coupe the large glass opening reveals a full-size spare mounted on a billet aluminum carrier.

Beneath the hood is a 4.6-liter V-8 with a Roots-type supercharger, enabling the engine to produce 400 horsepower and 390 ft-lb of torque. In the coupe, the engine is mated to a six-speed manual, while the convertible uses a five-speed automatic.

At the rear of the coupe, the dual exhaust exits through the bumper fascia, while the taillamps, which still retain their three-element look, extend nearly the entire length of the tail.

An overhead view of the GT convertible concept highlights a sport bar, a feature that won't make it into production. Also, for show purposes, the car has a row of toggle switches on the center dash. Adding considerable flash is an interior that makes extensive use of billet aluminum accents.

featured a large padded roll bar (it had no top), while the coupe sported an all-glass roof and a full-size spare proudly displayed under the glass hatch. Just as there would be no two-seat Mustang, the production version would come in a coupe instead of hatch.

"I think the concepts had some elements that were just fantastic in terms of modernity. I loved the hood scoops, and the side view was great," Mays says. In particular, the treatment of the side scoops and converting the coupe's quarter glass into air intakes caught Mays' eye. "If we could press metal that way, we would have done it in production. But we can't stamp out 160,000 cars a year with that kind of technical feel."

As nicely detailed as the concepts were, Mays still felt that some of the surfaces, particularly the hood, were too flat. "Just a bit more crown was needed to give the car more muscle," Mays says, adding that the hood didn't dive forward enough for the shark-nose look he wanted for the production car.

Another interesting detail at the rear of the concept car was the indentation above the taillights. Mays thought

The instruments feature highly technical detailing. The indicators are cogged gears that move around the face for a high-tech look.

*The shifter on the automatic-equipped Mustang GT convertible concept sits in front of a large boost gauge, with similarly geared readout as the speedometer and tach.*

it added a nice texture to the rear, but that such an execution in production would be difficult to do and compromise trunk space.

The interior, however, was a work of art. It had the toggle switches that Mays wanted and didn't have the corporate center stack of the production car. Instead there was a large boost gauge in the center console and large instruments with intricate, chronometer-inspired gauges. The doors had carbon fiber inserts, while the hard-back seats looked as if they came from a race car. Milled aluminum was everywhere: on the steering wheel, all over the dash, and on the console with a solid aluminum gated shifter. "How many millers milled for how many days to get that?" Mays muses, then adds that the vents "were too small to get any flow into the passenger compartment."

Beneath the hood of both Mustang GT concepts were supercharged 4.6-liter V-8s making 400 horsepower. The coupe was equipped with a six-speed manual, while the convertible had a five-speed automatic.

"We didn't need to go off and do these cars in terms of what we were doing with the production car," Mays says. "It did allow us to hold it up and get some feedback from the press and from consumers that we were headed down the right path. The cars gave Ford Division a lot of confidence that it had a winner on its hands."

"I think people liked the concepts, but they didn't love them like the production vehicles," Mays recalls. He notes that the convertible concept was actually pulled off the show circuit in fairly short order. "I heard over and over at this year's show that the production cars looked more muscular." In a perfect world, however, Mays would like to combine that more muscular look of the production cars with the more technical detailing of the concepts' surfacing.

The big question is, will the new Mustang stand the test of time? "It will be interesting to see the reaction not just for the first year or two—I'm interested in where this car is in people's minds four or five years into the cycle," Mays says. "That will tell the tale. Unlike the Thunderbird or the Beetle, I think this thing has some legs under it. It's too important a car to this country for people not to continue to embrace it."

One of the missions of the GT convertible concept was to emphasize the forward, shark-nose appearance of the 2005 Mustang.

While the concept features large instruments flanked by smaller gauges, in production the auxilliary readouts were positioned between the tach and speedometer.

# Four

# Ponies for the Pony

## Improving the Mustang's Drivetrain

"Few vehicles have been as closely identified with their engines over the years as the Mustang," he says. "Whether it was the Boss 302, the 351 Cleveland, the 5.0-liter or the 4.6-liter MOD engine, Mustang owners have always known—and bragged about—what was under the hood."

—Terry Wagner,

*Ford modular V-8/V-10 engine program manager*

*The rumble from the 2005 Mustang GT's dual exhaust announces the fact that there is 300 horsepower under the hood.*

MUCH OF THE MUSTANG'S ALLURE DERIVES FROM its muscular good looks. But those looks don't mean a thing if the car doesn't deliver the level of performance promised by the car's aggressive design.

With an established hierarchy of V-6, V-8, and supercharged V-8 powerplants, the Mustang team did not intend to change the existing lineup of engines, but rather sought to capitalize on the existing hardware, making significant revisions to bring performance to new levels.

Although the SVT Mustang Cobra went on hiatus when the new Mustang was launched at the end of 2004,

it's worthwhile to note the impact that the introduction of a 390-horsepower supercharged V-8 engine in 2003 had on drivetrain development for both the V-8 GT and V-6 models. Before supercharging, Cobra horsepower was in the 305 to 320 range (depending on model year), while the stock GT was somewhere around 250 to 260 horsepower, and the V-6 made 193 horsepower. When the first special-edition model of the GT, the Bullitt, hit the streets in 2001, it didn't offer a huge increase in power over the base GT, although torque response was much improved. If engineers had taken power up closer to

*The 4.6-liter V-8 engine has a new intake manifold and reworked three-valve heads to improve output. The engine retains its single serpentine belt system and features accessory drives that are bolted directly to the block.*

Cobra levels, it would have undermined sales of that premium model.

However, when the supercharged Cobra bowed with 390 horsepower, it opened up a significant gap between it and the GT. Consequently, when the Mustang Mach 1 went on sale in 2003, it could offer the SVT-tuned normally aspirated DOHC V-8 at 310 horsepower and not hurt Mustang Cobra sales.

The same was true for the all-new GT. With the coming of a new model, the Mustang team had the chance to do a major rework of the 4.6-liter Modular V-8 that had served so well since it replaced the 5.0-liter pushrod V-8 in 1996.

Terry Wagner, manager of the Ford Modular V-8/V-10 engine programs, outlined the opportunity that a new Mustang represented. "Consistent with our modular philosophy, we decided to evolve the 4.6-liter V-8," Wagner says. He explains that engines play a central role in the Mustang mystique, and lifting the hood to show off the engine is something that is not just expected but almost demanded of Mustang owners. "Few vehicles have been as closely identified with their engines over the years as the Mustang," he says. "Whether it was the Boss 302, the 351 Cleveland, the 5.0-liter or the 4.6-liter MOD engine, Mustang owners have always known—and bragged about—what was under the hood. With the new three-valve 4.6-liter MOD V-8, we're going to give them plenty to brag about again."

Best news is that for the first time, the standard GT—and not just a limited-production model like the SVT offering or the Mach 1—offers a full 300 horsepower and 315 ft-lb of torque, all from a less complex single overhead cam powerplant. The new engine puts out 40 more horses and 13 ft-lb more torque and incorporates many state-of-the-art advances such as electronic throttle control and variable valve timing. As a result of these high-tech three-valve heads, the new Mustang V-8 is a higher revver, producing peak power at 6,000 rpm and peak torque at 4,500 rpm, respective increases of 750 and 500 rpm. Redline on the new V-8 is 6,250 rpm.

"To get these levels of fuel economy, emissions, and performance, we need to get more flow by using two intake valves," Wagner notes. "Not only does it give us a greater percentage of torque and power over the two-valve engine, it delivers the same torque curve that you'll find on the current Mustang Mach 1's four-valve engine."

The V-8 engine program starts with the same modular block that was used on the previous Mustang. It is a deep-skirt design cast from aluminum, and it benefits from computer-aided design to beef up critical areas without adding unnecessary mass. Ford engineers estimated that a comparable cast-iron block would weigh 75 pounds more.

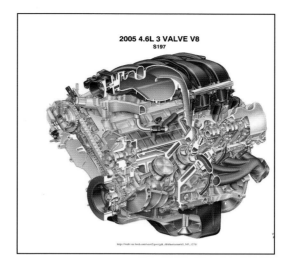

*This cutaway shows the internals of the revamped 4.6-liter V-8 engine. The intake charge travels through porting that induces a tumbling motion to more completely mix the air and fuel.*

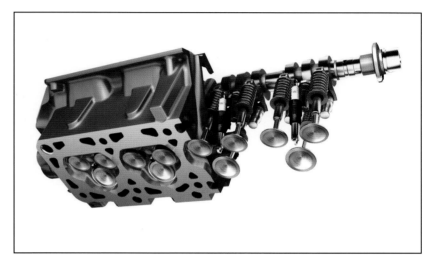

**The three-valve technology that allows the Mustang to reach the magic 300 horsepower level debuted on the new 2004 F-150 pickup. Note that the spark plug sits between the two intake valves.**

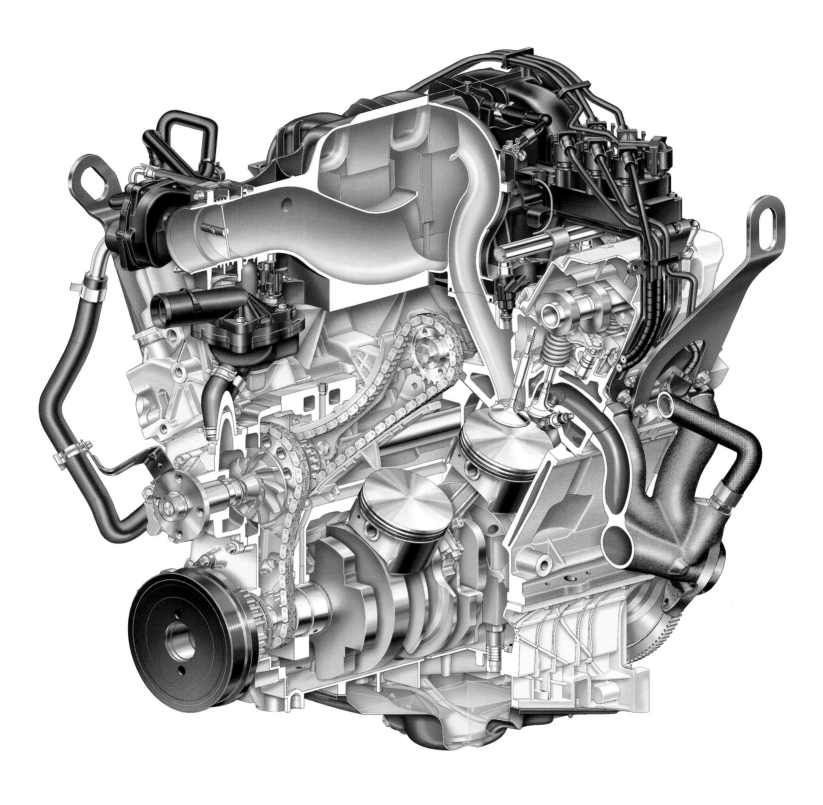

The base Mustang is equipped with a 60-degree V-6, displacing 4.0 liters and producing 210 horsepower. The SOHC engine is shared with the Ford Ranger and Explorer, although the Mustang has a different intake manifold.

All the block's internal parts are assembled with the tightest tolerances and the latest metals technology to reduce friction. The pistons are lightweight aluminum with short skirts and are coated with an anti-friction material. Each piston is fitted with high-tension rings that provide better sealing of the cylinder. This increases durability while reducing oil consumption. The connecting rods are made of powdered metal and have cracked caps for a more precise fit. The main bearings, called Select Fit, have their tolerances measured in microns rather than millimeters. The V-8 has five main cross-bolted bearings that feature bearing caps with trays attached to keep the oil fed to the crankshaft. This is particularly crucial when operating the car in high lateral load conditions.

While the bore diameter and stroke remains the same on the 4.6-liter V-8 (3.55x3.54 inches), the biggest change to the engine, which is largely responsible for the

bump in output, is the use of all-new three-valve heads with variable valve timing.

"The new three-valve engine is just plain clever," Wagner explains. "It enables optimization of horsepower, torque, fuel economy, and sound quality, and guarantees the engine always hits the sweet spot."

First of all, the new head provides a higher 9.8:1 compression ratio (up from 9.4:1) and yet the engine requires only 87-octane regular unleaded gas. The head is equipped with two intake valves that increase the volumetric efficiency of the engine, moving much more air in and out of the powerplant. Aiding in the scavenging of exhaust gases through the single valve is a tuned-length cast-iron exhaust manifold.

The head design, which includes a single overhead cam, allows for a center-mounted spark plug, which provides a symmetrical flame front for more complete

*An overhead view of the Mustang GT drivetrain shows this particular version equipped with the 5R55S five-speed automatic, which feeds power to the rear differential via a two-piece driveshaft. The dual exhaust features close-coupled catalytic converters for quick light-off and reduced cold-start emissions.*

burning of the fuel/air mixture. Using coil-on-plug electronic ignition, the plug itself is longer and narrower and extends deeper into the combustion chamber.

A more compact design than the previous two-valve heads, the new units provide a more direct air path to the intake valves, allowing better flow at higher engine rpms. The more compact size also leads to a slight weight reduction, thereby lowering the powertrain's center of gravity, a shift in weight that ultimately enhances the car's handling. Magnesium head covers not only reduce weight, but also are better sound insulators for the valvetrain.

The cams (one on each bank of cylinders) are equipped with low-profile roller-finger followers, which reduce friction and keep the overall engine height low. Variable valve timing allows up to 50 degrees of cam variation in relation to crankshaft angle, and the "dual-equal" timing shifts the opening of both intake and exhaust valves together, a simpler and less complex variable timing system than if intake and exhaust valves were adjusted separately. An electronic solenoid on the end of each cam modulates oil pressure to advance or retard valve timing as instructed by the engine's electronic controller.

## THE ELECTRONIC PONY

That electronic brain has gotten much smarter and now controls the throttle for the first time on the Mustang, eliminating the need for a mechanical link. "I can't emphasize enough how far we've come with our computer system," Wagner says. The primary sensor is located on the accelerator pedal and measures throttle angle, matching that information against engine speed and load. In turn, that information is used to adjust the 55-mm dual-bore throttle body to regulate engine speed.

The electronic throttle is also wired into the fuel injection system, cam timing, and, in cars equipped with the five-speed automatic, the electronic controller of the gearbox. This program, known as torque-based electronic throttle control, does more than just mimic a mechanical throttle linkage. It also adjusts fuel flow, valve action, and even gear changes to provide a more precise application of power. In addition, the electronic program, which is equipped with dual knock sensors, provides consistent engine performance in all temperatures and altitudes.

"The benefit of electronic throttle control to the driver is an effortless feeling that gives drivers more of what they want, when they want it," says Eric Levine, Mustang V-8 engine supervisor.

"This gives us a lot of capability to match the performance response of the car to the feel in your right foot," observes Wagner. At the same time, the electronic control "smoothes out the happy feet effects of someone who is constantly moving the throttle in and out" by finding a happy medium in throttle setting.

Redundancy is built into the electronic throttle control system through the use of extra sensors and double return springs at the accelerator, dual throttle body sensors, a closed-throttle-default actuator, and backup computing power with a diagnostic function. The Mustang is also equipped with a limp-home mode if there are multiple failures in the system.

An all-new intake manifold has been specially designed for the Mustang to ensure efficient handling of the air charge while providing a pleasing induction noise. In addition to the aforementioned 55-mm low-profile throttle body, the 4.6-liter V-8 is equipped with tuned intake runners that provide optimum torque at low engine revs and maximum horsepower at the top end of the rpm range. At low engine rpm, the air travels over a partially closed flap, called a Charge Motion Control Valve, which creates a slightly longer path to induce tumble in the flow. This turbulence leads to complete mixing of the air and fuel on its way to the combustion chamber. At higher engine revs, the valve opens up all the way, providing maximum airflow to the cylinder.

Even more important than the induction sound is the exhaust note coming out of the rear of the car. The V-8 is equipped with a true dual exhaust with closely coupled catalysts that quickly light off to control cold-start emissions. The exhaust travels through 2.5-inch Mandrel bent stainless-steel pipes. The twin exhaust has a center connector halfway back that allows communication between the two banks of cylinders, enabling engineers

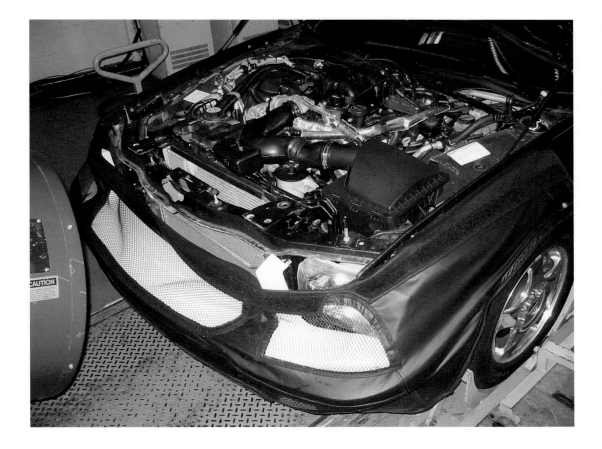

to tune the car for a throaty sound. The mufflers are bolted to the body aft of the rear axle for easy serviceability, and the exhaust exits through chromed tips.

## SIX TO GO

While six-cylinder Mustangs have been characterized as "secretaries' cars" since the car was launched in 1964, the new V-6 version offers more horsepower than the original 289-ci 200-horsepower V-8. The 2004 model's 3.8-liter 193-horsepower 90-degree pushrod V-6 has been supplanted by a 60-degree SOHC 4.0-liter V-6, which produces 210 horsepower at 5,250 rpm and 240 ft-lb of torque at 3,500 rpm, a gain of 10 ft-lb. Redline is pegged at 6,100 rpm.

"The V-6 is a big player in the Mustang segment," Chuck Gray, engine manager for the V-6, explains. "It represents two-thirds of the volume. What I love about the new engine is the increased output and the sound quality. Now you not only get the new Mustang styling, but the V-6 packs a more visceral punch as well."

The V-6 has a cast-iron block and aluminum heads with a bore and stroke of 3.95x3.32 inches. Like the V-8, it uses aluminum pistons but instead of cracked powdered metal for the connecting rods, it uses forged steel. The compression ratio is 9.7:1 and like the V-8, it operates on 87-octane unleaded regular.

The engine block also features a girdled crankcase for increased strength and rigidity, a dual-mode crankshaft dampener, and composite cam covers to reduce noise, vibration, and harshness.

Although the 4.0-liter V-6 is shared with the Ford Ranger, a composite intake system was designed specifically for use in the Mustang. The engine is also equipped with new tuned-length exhaust manifolds, flywheel, and oil pan. The engine's cooling circuit was redesigned and the engine fitted with a new exhaust gas recirculation (EGR) system and enhanced fuel injection to reduce evaporative leakage.

The new 60-degree V-6 does have a slightly taller profile than the 90-degree V-6 it replaces, but it benefits

**Much attention has been lavished on the underhood presentation of the 4.6-liter V-8. The intake manifold is embossed with the galloping pony, and the snorkel for the twin throttle bodies has an elegant wrap that allows free air flow.**

from the use of low-profile heads with the cams driven by a slave shaft mounted low in the engine's "V." Like the V-8, this allows for a lower overall engine profile and lowers the drivetrain's center of gravity. Equipped with electronic sequential fuel injection, the two-valve V-6 has a 65-mm single-bore throttle body and uses a coil pack for ignition without a distributor.

Both the V-8 and V-6 engines use liquid-filled engine mounts on both sides of the engine. These hydro-mount bushings are specifically tuned to filter out unwanted engine vibration.

Extensive research has gone into the exhaust note of the V-6, including internal and outside clinics on sound quality. Overall, the goal was to provide a note that sounds powerful without being overpowering. The debate on just how loud the V-6 should be continued up until the final engineering sign-offs six months prior to launch. Even with this last-minute fine-tuning, there was no doubt that the new V-6 would sound much more muscular than the car it replaces.

In keeping with the muscle car image the Mustang seeks to project, both the GT and V-6 models are equipped with a Tremec five-speed manual transmission as standard equipment. The V-8 model is equipped with the beefier Tremec 3650 that features taller and slightly closer gear ratios than the V-6 model, which uses the tried-and-true T5 gearbox. The V-8 has a 3.38:1 first gear, 2.00:1 second, and 1.32:1 third, compared to the T5's respective ratios of 3.35:1, 1.99:1, and 1.33:1. Both gearboxes have a direct-drive fourth and a 0.68:1 overdrive fifth. The V-8's snappiness off the line is enhanced by its 3.55:1 final drive, while V-6 models use a more modest 3.31:1 final ratio, which is similar to the differentials used in all automatics. The GT has a traction-lock 8.8-inch rear axle, while the V-6 has a 7.5-inch ring-and-pinion set.

Both the 3650 and T5 include upgrades to make the shift throws smoother and more precise, and the clutch features a hydraulic boost to reduce effort. Another change is the use of flanged coupling instead of splined drive to connect the driveshaft to the gearbox. The V-6 has new clutch plate material to enhance durability, while the clutch disc on the V-8 has a larger diameter to handle the additional engine output.

The GT model is equipped with a two-piece driveshaft in order to handle the higher engine speeds and torque, while the V-6 has a slip-in-tube single piece unit.

A five-speed automatic is offered for the first time as an option on both the GT and V-6 Mustangs. The 5R55S gearbox, which is also used on the Lincoln LS and Ford Thunderbird, has closely spaced ratios to improve acceleration. Both cars share the same gearing with a 3.22:1 first, 2.29:1 second, and 1.54:1 third gear. Fourth is direct drive and fifth is a 0.71:1 overdrive. As mentioned earlier, this gearbox is tied closely into the engine control module, which governs shift duration and timing. A new electronic interface allows the gearbox to communicate with the electronic control module 10 times faster than before, allowing for near real-time adjustments of the shift points to match throttle inputs and valve timing.

With 300 horsepower on tap, getting that power down to the rear wheels in less than ideal conditions is a challenge met by the standard traction control system on all GT models (the V-6 adds traction control as an option

*Just enough slip is programmed into the Mustang's traction control system to allow smoky burnouts.*

bundled with ABS). By using the same high-speed electronic network that serves the drive-by-wire system, the traction control program monitors both engine performance and wheel slip detected by the ABS sensors. The system is configured to determine, by the amount of slip detected, whether the vehicle is on dry or wet pavement and in turn uses a combination of braking and retarding the throttle to regain grip.

When the system detects dry pavement, the intervention is not as immediate or aggressive, allowing the tires to spin or the tail to hang out slightly in spirited driving. However, once excess slip is detected, either through excessive vehicle yaw or the wheels spinning up at a faster rate (which would indicate a slippery surface), traction control reacts quickly and decisively to bring the spinning wheel back in check.

There also is a switch to disable and rearm the traction control system, which is easily accessible on the center stack (and not hidden away in the glove box). It automatically resets itself to engage traction control each time the ignition is cycled off.

This high-tech approach to engine management enables the Mustang to deliver better fuel economy and lower emissions. And yet, the sound coming from the back end of the car, from the exhaust note to the squealing tires, is better than ever.

# A New Home for the Pony

The 2005 Mustang marks the beginning of a new era for this American icon. The Mustang will be built in a new home for the first time in its 40-year history. The move to the 2-million-square-foot factory at AutoAlliance International (AAI), some 15 miles away from its Dearborn origins in Flat Rock, Michigan, represents another milestone for Mustang: it will be built alongside a different vehicle.

The front-wheel-drive Mazda 6 will travel down the same final assembly line as the rear-wheel-drive Mustang. AAI is a joint venture between Ford and Mazda, the latter of which Ford owns a controlling share.

The irony that the Mustang's new home is where the front-wheel-drive Probe was produced (destined at one time to be the Mustang's successor) is not lost on AAI's president, Phil Spender. "The workers have felt all along that they could do a great job on the Mustang, and they're excited to finally get the 'real' one in here."

Moving Mustang to a plant where it shares production with another model is crucial to the car's survival. Sales of specialty coupes like the Mustang have peaks and valleys. Having another product to build alongside the Mustang ensures the plant will remain productive during periods of slack demand.

*Freshly stamped parts are taken out of one of three on-site presses and loaded into racks.*

"The secret is to build at high overall volume and yet build to demand," Spender says. The product mix at AAI is highly complex. In addition to the Mustang coupe and convertible, the plant produces the Mazda 6 in three variants: four-door sedan, five-door hatchback, and station wagon. Added to this are two engine and transmission choices for the Mustang (V-6 and V-8 manual and automatic) and two for the Mazda 6 (I-4 and V-6 manual and automatic).

Later on, AAI will add to its mix the SVT Mustang Cobra with independent rear suspension, and specialty models like the Mach 1 and Bullitt. This complexity is one of the reasons AAI was chosen over several other assembly plants in the Ford system.

"Three years ago, we defined our role as being a sporty car factory," Spender says. The "Zoom Zoom" nature of the Mazda product, he adds, means that the cars have different wheels, tires, and trim packages that range from standard base cars to highly-equipped sport sedans. "We have to have flexibility to quickly change wheel and tire packages and have a wide range of engine and transmission flexibility," Spender notes. "This was a decision we made with the Mustang in mind."

The ability to manufacture such disparate products as the front-wheel-drive Mazda 6 station wagon and the rear-wheel-drive Mustang Cobra with independent rear suspension is almost without precedent in the auto industry. Even at the

*Body panels are moved directly from the stamping plant to assembly, where robotic arms weld Mustang bodies together.*

*Within the AutoAlliance facility there are two separate welding lines, one for the Mustang and the other for the Mazda 6. Here, Mustang bodies move down the line where doors will be attached and then sequenced with Mazdas in the paint shop.*

Dearborn Assembly Plant, which was dedicated to Mustang production, the SVT Cobras were batch-built. At AAI, they will come down the same line interspersed with Mazda 6s and Mustang GTs.

At full capacity, the plant produces between 260,000 and 300,000 Mustang and Mazda 6 models annually on two shifts, employing approximately 3,500 workers. It takes just under 60 hours for a Mustang to go from body framing to completion. Spender says at peak production, 74 cars per hour roll off the assembly line.

AAI boasts its own stamping plant for body panels and major structural components. Four gigantic presses operate around the clock on three shifts.

"The key to the stamping plant is that we make all the parts that give us the final dimensions and fits of the vehicle," Spender explains. "If gaps or fits fall out of spec, they can be quickly addressed at the source in the plant, rather than having a fix work its way back through the supply chain."

The Dearborn Assembly Plant was built in 1918 to build ships. Later, it produced a series of cars, including the Model A, and became Mustang's home in 1964. This facility has tremendous history but looks every bit its age in comparison to the 15-year-old AAI facility. The Flat Rock facility has high ceilings, a light and airy work space, and the latest in equipment, such as overhead carriers and skids that adjust up and down to allow all the workers to perform their tasks standing up and at chest level. The wood-covered conveyor belt (the wood makes it easier to stand for long periods) carries the workers along with the cars as they perform their tasks. These ergonomics reduce fatigue and ensure consistent and high-quality assembly.

There are two main buildings on the site, one of which is a huge facility that accepts 4,000 components from over 400 suppliers and sequences all the parts for proper installation. This building also has several smaller lines that assemble modular subsystems like the instrument panel and the rear axle. AAI adheres to the philosophy of lean manufacturing. Inventory is kept at a minimum for just-in-time deliveries of components on the assembly line.

The main building consists of four wings, one housing the stamping plant, another the body shop, a third the paint shop, and the fourth is home to final assembly. Body parts for both the Mustang and Mazda 6 are stamped out in the same plant but sent to their own specific lines for framing and welding. Once the unpainted bodies are mated with doors and hoods, the two lines come together. The Ford and Mazda products share the same paint and final assembly lines.

Advanced paint shop technology enables AAI to paint both makes of cars in colors specific to their brands in the same spray booth, although there are basic colors like black and white that are shared.

The level of automation is high in the plant, especially in dangerous areas like the body shop, where robotic arms do virtually all the welding.

*An interior buck carved from billet aluminum is used to precisely measure the fit of interior components like the dashboard and center console.*

While the pounding thuds of the stamping presses or the flying sparks from the welding line are dramatic manifestations of a car being built, the real heavy lifting in the production process happens in a small, nondescript corner of the plant called the "Dimensional Control Area." Here, bodies are measured against a perfect template to determine where variations are occurring in the assembly process to ensure that seams and panel fits are uniform. Another dimensional tool in this area is an interior buck that replicates the body of the Mustang. Carved out of billet aluminum, this fixture is used to test how well interior components like the modular dash, center console, and seats line up in the Mustang. Spender believes these are some of the most critical fits on the car because most of the time a Mustang owner spends with the car is behind the wheel looking at the dash and interior trim.

Back on the assembly line, Spender says most of the build, which includes doors-off interior trimming, is fairly straightforward for both the Mustang and the Mazda 6. Things don't get tricky until the glass is installed, which is now an automated operation, and the drivetrain is mated to the body.

The glass-installing station had to be enlarged and additional machines put in to accommodate the Mustang. Sensors identify the body style, and robot arms swoop down to pick out the correct glass pieces, on which workers have manually applied sealer. The arms gently lift and press the glass into place.

On the other side of the aisle from this operation the drivetrain is mated to the chassis. On the Mazda products, the front engine cradle and axle, along with the rear suspension, are lifted into place. Mustangs only receive their drivetrain and front suspension. The line moves down and doubles back to the next aisle where the rear

Left and next page: *Bodies are randomly pulled from the assembly line and all tolerances checked to ensure a quality build.*

suspension and two-piece driveshaft on Mustangs are installed while the rear suspension on the Mazdas is tightened down.

When the cars roll off the final assembly line, Mustang convertibles are singled out for additional checks, adjustments, and water tests to ensure that the tops fit snugly.

Outside the plant, AAI has the advantage of its own test track where random models are test driven to quickly ferret out problems.

"People joke around that we built this track to have fun during lunch," Spender says, laughing.

"Actually, this track significantly helps us improve efficiency and quality since we can build, drive, analyze, and fix cars or processes with all of the key players at one location."

AAI has a long, proud history of building cars for both Mazda and Ford that continues with the joint production of the Mustang and the Mazda 6. "The AAI joint venture between Ford and Mazda is one of the best examples of flexible manufacturing," Spender proudly points out. "We knew this would be the perfect new home for the Mustang."

*A completed car drives through an area called the Great Hall, which links the body shop, paint facility, and final assembly hall.*

# Five

# Agility Rules

## Making the Best Handling Mustang Ever

"The new car is clearly the best steering and handling Mustang GT ever built. I can tell you that with confidence."

—*Mark Rushbrook,*
*Ford vehicle development manager*

**The 2005 Mustang retains a traditional solid rear axle but with a twist. The new three-link setup offers improved handling without the added expense or weight of an independent suspension.**

S TRAIGHT-LINE THRILLS ARE EXPECTED from the Mustang. While that remains one of the car's endearing virtues, times have changed. Cars have evolved. The joy of driving comes not just from the rush of acceleration, but also from the ability to conquer twisting bits of road in spirited fashion. Good handling is a given. And just because the spec sheet says "solid axle" doesn't mean the Mustang is a throwback to the days when passengers were told, "Sit down, shut up, and hang on." Instead, the Mustang combines the quickness of a traditional muscle car with the surefootedness of a modern sports car.

Phil Martens, Ford group vice president of product creation, stressed that straight-line performance and refined road manners are necessary ingredients to the car's success. "Mustang is all about driving," Martens says. "The Mustang's all-new chassis design does everything better—accelerates, turns, stops—while isolating unwanted noise and making the most of the powerful new engine. It's a complete driving experience."

While the platform is unique to Mustang, the MacPherson strut front suspension is similar to that used on the Lincoln LS. Certainly cost concerns favor the less expensive strut setup over double wishbone or short- and long-arm independent front suspensions. But purists take heart. The design is similar to that used on the legendary BMW M3. As BMW has proven time and again, executing a simple design deftly can work as well or better than more complex and costly bits. It's a lesson the Mustang team has taken to heart.

The coil-over MacPherson strut has reverse L-shaped lower control arms made of stamped steel formed into I-beam sections. The result is a suspension component that is extremely stiff and lightweight, lighter than a cast-aluminum piece with the same stiffness. This contributes to a reduction in unsprung weight.

Through his racing experience, Mark Rushbrook, Mustang vehicle development manager, knows a thing or two about the pitfall of extra weight in suspension components. "Having too much unsprung weight is like trying to play basketball in ski boots," he explains.

"Keeping unsprung weight low gives the suspension the quickness to stay firmly planted to the road."

The L-shaped control arm has the advantage of using the shorter forward leg with stiff bushings to control side-to-side motion, which also aids steering response. The longer leg of the L, positioned longitudinally, is attached to a softer fluid-filled bushing. The long leg has greater leverage working against a softer mount readily absorbing road shocks, thereby improving the ride without sacrificing taut handling.

The front tubular steel stabilizer bar, which measures 34 mm on the GT and 28.6 mm on the V-6, has a unique link that ties the low-mounted bar to the mounting base of the springs. This provides a direct counterforce in cornering to reduce body roll, rather than sending the forces through the frame rails.

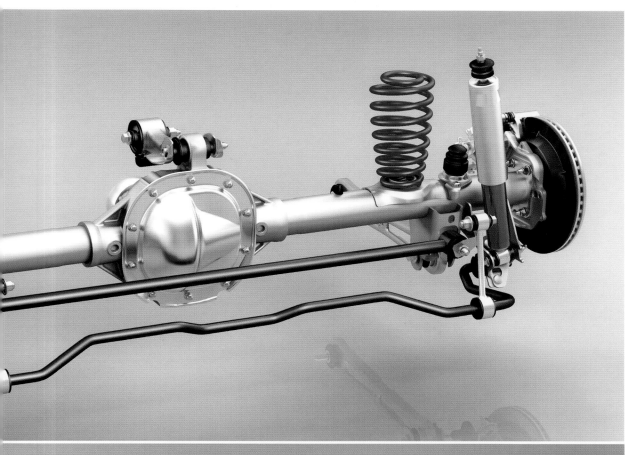

In addition to three links, the rear axle is equipped with a Panhard rod that adds torsional stiffness to prevent rear-end hop under hard cornering.

The front suspension has MacPherson struts with coil-over springs. The springs are made of high-strength steel, which allows them to be 44 percent lighter.

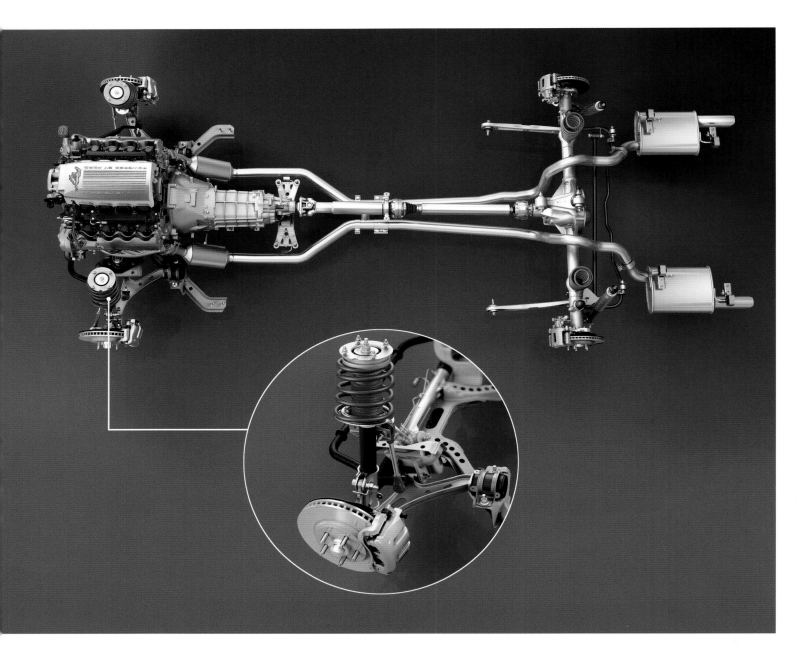

*This close-up of the front suspension shows the L-shaped lower link that is formed into an I-beam using stamped steel pieces making it extremely stiff, yet light in weight.*

Nestled between the MacPherson struts is a new, power-assisted rack-and-pinion steering unit that is lighter and more responsive. With a faster 15.7:1 ratio over the 2004's 15.0:1 setup, the steering has crisper turn-in and reduces the turning circle nearly 3 feet over the last generation's 37.1-foot distance.

While the front suspension is considered state-of-the-art, some may view the rear solid axle design with skepticism, which is understandable if you've had any experience with rigid axles suspended by leaf springs. Those springs typically have a difficult time controlling axle

hop under full throttle acceleration and offer little in the way of lateral control in high-speed handling. However, solid axle technology has evolved and the 2005 Mustang takes this tried-and-true technology to a higher level.

Chris Dorros, a suspension engineer on the Mustang team, says durability, light weight, and low cost were prime objectives in the design of the rear suspension, with an eye on what modifications customers make on their own, whether their interests lie in road racing or drag-strip action.

"Our biggest challenge and biggest success was making this suspension tough yet easy to modify for the

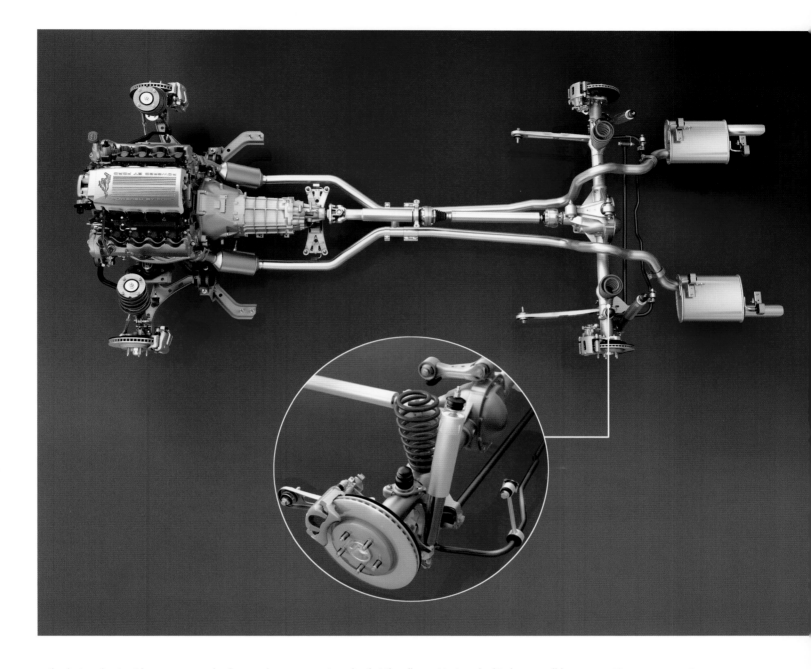

enthusiast, and yet not heavy or expensive for people who just wanted to enjoy the ride," Dorros says. "One of Mustang's greatest strengths is how it appeals to everyone. You can't change that. And we also never forgot that our part was just a piece of the whole car. You have to keep the entire system in mind to make it work."

Hau Thai-Tang, Mustang chief engineer, reveals that customer input helped settle the decision on the rear suspension. "We talked to a lot of Mustang owners when we were developing this program. They are a very passionate group and a lot of them told us—very

strongly—that the all-new Mustang had to have a solid rear axle," he says.

But it wouldn't be just any old solid rear axle. Instead, the suspension team came up with a new three-link design aided by a center-mounted Panhard rod to locate the rear axle. The differential casing is 20 percent stiffer, which adds to the overall solid feel. The axle is mounted on two outboard trailing links. A third upper control arm, with specially calibrated bushings, is mounted to the top of the differential. This single arm link is positioned on the vehicle's centerline for reduced

*The rear suspension uses outboard-mounted shocks to improve ride performance and provide additional lateral support.*

friction and is set vertically to provide 60 percent more leverage against axle windup. The result is smooth and consistent launches.

The Panhard rod, which is mounted to the body parallel to the rear of the axle, attaches behind the two rear links and improves side-to-side control of the axle in hard cornering. Constant-rate coil springs are mounted directly on top of the axle, while the shocks are located outboard and to the rear of the axle. The outboard mounting of the shocks reduces the lever effect of the axle and permits a softer damping rate to improve ride. The coil springs directly link the axle housing to the body and have constant rates for a linear response.

GT models are equipped with a 22-mm solid rear stabilizer bar that uses body-mounted swing links to reduce unsprung weight.

Unlike previous Mustangs, which used fewer suspension components to manage the many forces working on the solid axle, the 2005 Mustang has more links and a more complex geometry to address these forces individually. This allows for custom-tuned bushings and more precise control of axle movement. The design maintains constant track, toe-in, and camber relative to the road surface, and it keeps body roll under control. Road impacts are isolated and damped while the use of the Panhard rod provides solid lateral control to improve

stability over mid-corner bumps. Overall, the rear end, despite using what is considered old technology, feels as planted as most independent rear suspensions and yet is less costly, lighter, and more robust.

Wheel and tire packages optimize the suspension on the Mustang and deliver the necessary grip to keep up with the suspension's capabilities. The GT is equipped

*The engine bay features a crossmember that is 33 percent lighter and is designed to dissipate the energy from crash forces. Hydraulic-filled bushings used in engine mounting reduce vibration and harshness.*

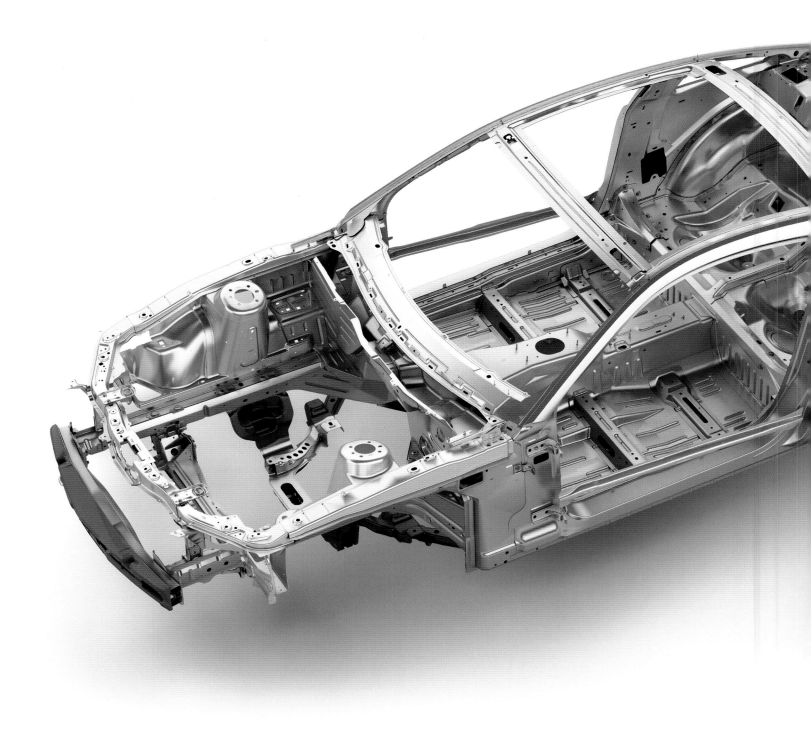

with standard 17x8-inch alloy wheels shod with Pirelli P235/55ZR17 W-rated all-season tires. The V-6 models have 16x7-inch alloy wheels wearing S-rated BFGoodrich P215/65R16 tires. The GT sports five-spoke wheels, while the V-6 has a 10-spoke pattern. The relatively tall profile of the tires, especially on the V-6 models, helps fill the Mustang's flared arches.

Behind those wheels are four-wheel disc brakes that are larger in diameter than previous models. The GT benefits from 12.4-inch front and 11.8-inch rear rotors that

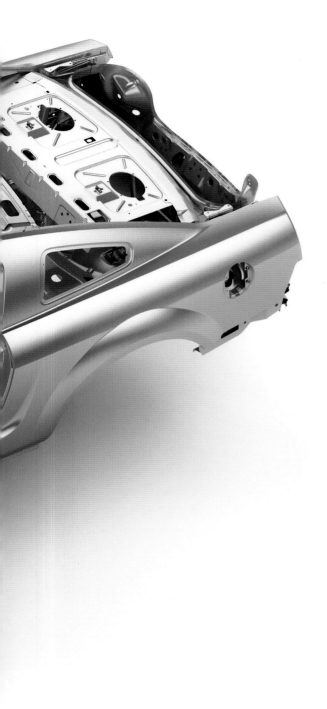

front rotors and the same 11.8-inch by 19-millimeter vented rear discs. Both models use twin-piston, 43-millimeter floating aluminum calipers on the front and single pot 43-millimeter floating iron calipers on the rear.

Electronic brake force distribution automatically modulates the clamping force, applying it where it's most needed. Four-channel ABS is standard on the GT and an available option on the V-6. The stiff construction of the brakes and increased swept area provides shorter stopping, better pedal feel, and longer life for the brake components.

## THE STRONG, SILENT TYPE

While good handling and powerful braking contribute greatly to active safety, a stiff body structure is essential to managing crash forces in an accident. And that stiffness is also crucial in building a solid foundation from which the chassis works. The all-new Mustang allowed engineers to develop a body that goes far beyond the torsion levels the previous team was able to achieve with its inherited Fox platform.

Keith Knudsen, Mustang package supervisor, explains that the ground-up approach to body and package design helped to create a structure that is both roomy and protective of its occupants.

"The tallest drivers in our customer base have not been fully happy with the previous Mustangs," Knudsen admits. "We've addressed that in this all-new car while maintaining the 'cockpit feel' essential to a driver's car. But we wanted to improve comfort for passengers, too. The extra cabin space makes a world of difference on long drives."

The increase in cabin space resulted in 1/2 inch more headroom for the driver and a 1.8-inch increase in shoulder room. As a result, the front seats aren't as closely coupled as they were in the previous car. The 5.8-inch increase in wheelbase to 107.1 inches translates to 1.1 inches more legroom for the rear seat occupants. Also in the rear, passengers will find 1.2 inches more shoulder room.

But increased room is just the first step. Improving the safety and the handling of the car is directly attributed to the strength of the body structure. "The foundation for

*An all-new body structure is 31 percent stiffer than the 2004 Mustang. The front rails on the body have an octagonal shape that spreads crash forces evenly across the firewall.*

have respective swept areas of 64.3 square inches and 49.7 square inches, an increase of 15 percent overall. The vented discs have a thickness of 30-millimeter front and 19-millimeter rear. The V-6, due to its slightly lighter curb weight, has smaller 30-millimeter-thick 11.5-inch vented

*Much of the early chassis development was done using two previous-generation Mustangs known as Chip (a convertible) and Dale (a coupe). While Chip looked more stock, Dale's hood was cobbled together to provide additional underhood clearance.*

the new Mustang is a high-strength steel body shell that's completely new," Knudsen says. "It's safe and secure, and it has outstanding driving dynamics that help drivers avoid accidents in the first place."

Most drivers know from seat-of-the-pants experience when body integrity is high. Often, comments are heard that a car seems as if it is carved from a solid billet of metal or that it feels as secure as a vault. Engineers have a way of measuring the torsion rigidity of a body, and in the new Mustang they've found that it takes 15,500 ft-lb of force to deform the body by one degree. In other words, the structure is 31 percent stiffer than the car it replaces.

And yet, while the body needs this rigid construction to make the car handle as a single unit, it must have forgiving crumple zones to absorb crash impacts in order to protect the vehicle's occupants. Up front are frame rails that manage this energy in a controlled crush. These pieces have an octagon shape that prevents buckling, thereby allowing them to progressively deform and spread the forces out evenly across the firewall. This also provides increased protection in offset front crashes. Leftover energy is transferred into the safety cage surrounding the passenger compartment. The No. 2 crossmember, which helps to manage front impact forces, is also 33 percent lighter and yet stronger thanks to the use of high-strength steel.

Another challenge in developing the body was adapting split folding rear seats to the design for the first time. This eliminated the rear bulkhead, but additional bracing in the package shelf and along the floor beneath the rear seat contributes to the improvements in the torsion stiffness of the new car.

As the body engineers developed the Mustang's structure, particular attention was paid to the natural vibrating frequencies of the various components. Using computers, the interior was mapped to pinpoint hot spots where road noise, drivetrain vibration, and suspension harshness could be transmitted into the passenger compartment. The parts were either redesigned or additional soundproofing applied to ensure low noise levels inside. Yet, care was taken not to filter out road feel and the exhaust note that gives the Mustang its sporty character.

Inside, passengers are protected with dual-stage front airbags capable of deploying at full or partial power, depending on the speed of the impact. A sensor uses the weight of the passenger to determine the proper inflation rate for the airbag. If no weight or very little weight is detected, the bag is automatically switched off. If there is weight similar to that of a small child, the bag remains deactivated and a light goes on warning that the bag is disabled. If an adult is occupying the seat, the airbag is armed and ready to deploy. The seatbelts also utilize pyrotechnic pretensioners to take up slack within milliseconds if a crash occurs.

## TO HELL AND BACK

Well, actually, to Unadilla and back. The development team spent countless hours driving, evaluating, and tuning the chassis and body in a series of weekly real-world excursions over twisty two-lane highways near Hell, Michigan, a rural area 60 miles northwest of Detroit. The so-called Unadilla Loop, which goes through a wide spot

in the road of the same name, provided Team Mustang members a chance to get out of their offices and garages to test improvements to the car's suspension, brakes, steering, body tuning, critical noise, vibration, and harshness damping.

Of course, much of this work preceded the actual drives where team members would use computer-aided design and engineering technology to model all the suspension components and how they would fit together and react to each other. This advance work shaved months off the development time, allowing engineers to try countless variations and eliminate the obvious setups that wouldn't work well.

Once the hardware had been sufficiently developed, it was time to make prototypes, and many of the cars have been extensively tested on racetracks, proving grounds, and hot and cold weather testing sites around the world.

"We spent countless hours refining this car on development drives and at the track," Vehicle Development

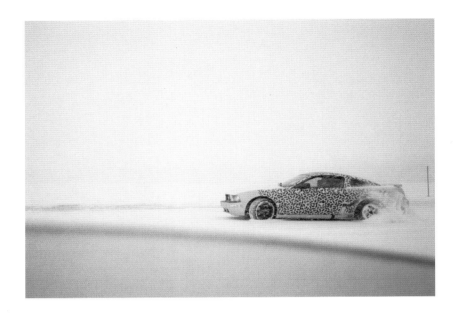

*Mustangs logged more than 20,000 test days and 1,000,000 miles of cold-weather driving. Here a mule performs a snowy burnout at the Dearborn Proving Grounds.*

Manager Mark Rushbrook explains. "The car has been to the Nelson Ledges road course in Ohio several times for 24-hour runs and has spent months on our straightaways and handling courses at our proving grounds in Arizona, Michigan, and Florida."

This type of development work is the glamour part of the business, the kind enthusiasts dream of. Who wouldn't want to drive the new Mustang as fast as it can go around tracks and proving grounds?

But far more important is the rather mundane driving done on the Unadilla Loop. The process began with early prototypes that melded the new Mustang's underpinnings with the previous car's bodywork; the only distinguishing characteristics were the extended front fenders that accommodate the new car's longer wheelbase and wider track. Engineer's called the first such prototype "Chip" and its partner car "Dale" after the Disney chipmunks. As development progressed, cars with more representative bodywork camouflaged in black-and-white leopard decals replaced them. Later, after the production car had been shown at the 2004 North American International Auto Show, completely undisguised prototypes cruised as unobtrusively as they could over the Unadilla Loop at the posted speed limits, which range from 35 to 55 miles per hour.

Each circuit of the Unadilla Loop takes roughly 15 to 20 minutes, with the driver swapping either into another variation of the Mustang or a competitive car. The cars circulated monotonously; the drivers took notes, both written and mental, on what they felt from the steering, the brakes, the ease with which the shifter worked, interior noise levels, and even the exhaust note.

Sometimes the rides were organized around a particular set of "issues" or problems that needed to be worked through. It could be the sound of the V-6 engine, seat comfort, or airflow through the ventilation system. Other times the evaluations were much broader, soliciting general impressions and performing check rides in advance of major engineering sign-offs.

"Our job is to balance all the attributes—like ride, handling, and steering—and make sure our customers feel free when they are behind the wheel of a new Mustang," says Rushbrook. "The new car is clearly the best steering and handling Mustang GT ever built. I can tell you that with confidence."

A typical session would consist of three hours of what is best described as everyday driving, after which the team reassembled around a table to debrief. Representatives of the major subsystems were all present, ready to report the findings back to their groups to make changes or investigate further to come up with empirical data to back or counter the subjective impressions of the test drivers.

Bob Johnston, vehicle engineering manager and technical advisor to chief engineer Hau Thai-Tang, presided over many of the sessions, making sure that all the issues that arose were addressed. These meetings were tense, with various disciplines sensitive to criticisms, and everyone trying to do the best they can within time and cost constraints. A better description, though, would be intense. With the cars parked right outside the meeting room, engineers had instant access and could jump into the cars for a quick drive to point out concerns. By the time the engineers returned to the meeting, they often saw eye-to-eye.

And sometimes, Johnston himself went to great lengths to identify an issue. On one predawn drive along the Unadilla Loop, Johnston and Rushbrook thought they had picked up on a noise coming from the rear axle.

Johnston jumped into the trunk, while Rushbrook drove the loop again. "I bet a lot of people think about putting their boss in the trunk," Rushbrook quipped. To which Johnston replied, "Our trunk is pretty large for a performance car. Try jumping into the back of a GTO."

Johnston believed that the open exchange of the meetings and the ability to pinpoint early-on conflicting objectives led to the best solutions.

"I feel like I'm the court of appeals," Johnston said at the time. "When some members of the team wanted to increase the suspension rates for vehicle dynamics and others wanted to reduce the rates for noise, vibration, and harshness, I helped decide where the balance needed to be. There are great expectations of what this car should be, great understanding of what this car has been, and a fiercely passionate group of loyalists that you can't afford to disappoint."

*Cars with bodywork representative of the new design were camouflaged in black-and-white leopard decals during testing on the Unadilla loop.*

# Behind the Wheel

## Experiencing the Mustang From the Driver's Seat

Once you slip behind the wheel of the 2005 Mustang GT, there's no mistaking the fact that the car is totally new.

*Even though they share the same bodies, the detailing on the Mustang GT and V-6 models differs to reflect the character of their different drivetrains.*

THERE MAY BE ONLY ONE MUSTANG, BUT WITH THE 2005 model Ford has managed to produce a car with two distinct personalities: the muscular V-8 GT and the sporty yet refined V-6 coupe.

Mustang Chief Engineer Hau Thai-Tang explains the personality is a reflection of specific market segments that the car serves. "We have our Cobra which is the king of the line, the V-6 which covers the entry level, and the GT, as well as what we call buzz products like the Mach 1 and Bullitt. Without getting into specifics, the Cobra will be moved up further in performance, which gives us more room to move the GT up. The GT is a significantly better car all around than the previous model."

This new personality is much bolder and starts with aggressive styling.

"The shape telegraphs that this is a muscular sports car," Thai-Tang says. "We want the drive experience to build on that look. The horsepower and torque are raised significantly. The steering and handling make it very rewarding for the enthusiast driver and make it easy to drive for the novice. The key thing about the Mustang is

that anybody looks good in one. It's a car that appeals to all generations. But more than just looking good, we want everyone to drive well in a Mustang."

The GT's bold, in-your-face styling starts with the large driving lights nestled in the grille. The large lower fascia's four-segment intake complements the GT's aggressive face. The sides of the vehicle have rocker extensions, which pull the body sides lower to the ground, while the large 17-inch wheel and tire package fills up the wheelwells.

From head on, the GT has a muscular, purposeful stance. The fenders look like a bodybuilder's arms curved over the wheels, while the front end, with its bold array of lights and galloping pony badge, seems to sneer at onlookers. If you look closely into the outboard headlamp bezels, you can see two small gills that pay homage to the earlier Mustangs that had similar vents on their noses.

Beneath the headlamps are the turn signal indicators, mounted in a recess that carries around the front corner and directly into the wheelwell arch for a smooth transition that gives the car the look that it has

been sculpted from a single piece of metal. The strength of the body is reinforced with visual cues that include sharply creased character lines and strong shoulders. The side scallop is framed by a single line that curves up like a hockey stick and blends smoothly into the body instead of terminating at the door handle high side crease. The 17-inch alloy wheels are offered in two five-spoke styles: a standard, gray painted mag wheel and an optional polished aluminum wheel with split spokes. After the initial launch, an 18-inch dished and polished five-spoke wheel was added to the option list.

Contrasting with the sharp-edged surfacing of the body, the rear quarter glass has rounded corners for balance. The B-pillar has a rearward rake adding to the fastback effect of the car's profile.

From behind, the aggressiveness of the GT is reinforced with the rear spoiler and a large rear fascia with two cutouts to showcase the chrome-tipped dual exhaust. The high-mounted stop light is located in the trailing edge of the deck lid, which allows for an unobstructed view out the rear window. A large GT badge, which houses the

*The GT can be specified with seats that contrast with the interior, like these red buckets or black seats with red inserts. The aluminum trim dominates the dash, while the steering wheel has a retro three-spoke look.*

*As a result of the longer wheelbase over the previous car, rear seat passengers enjoy greater legroom, while the split-fold seat back—a new feature for the Mustang—increases the flexibility of the car's load-carrying capability.*

trunk's keyhole, is flanked by the trademark three-segment taillamps. Other GT badges can be found on the front fenders.

To differentiate the V-6 coupe from its more muscular V-8 sibling, its design is simpler and, in a way, more elegant in execution. In addition to dispensing with the grille-mounted auxiliary lighting, the V-6 coupe has a smaller and slimmer front bumper with a smaller lower

intake divided into just three segments. A front license plate pocket breaks the bumper line. The V-6 shares the same headlamp bezels with gill detailing inside the lighting can.

The V-6 model is leaner, yet no less athletic in appearance. In profile, the V-6 is distinguished by its black rocker panels which give the impression that the body curves beneath the car higher off the ground. The 10-

spoke, 16-inch alloy wheels (in standard trim they are painted silver-gray, while optional two-tone alloys with the same design sport fake knock-off hubs) are fitted with taller profile tires. The black rocker panels and taller tires make the V-6 coupe look much lighter on its feet than the hunkered down GT. At the rear, a cutout for the single exhaust tip on the right side identifies the V-6, as does the rear badge sporting the galloping pony. Without the rear wing, the tail of the V-6 coupe is clean and modern. Optional Mustang decals and an add-on spoiler give the V-6 a bit of a retro boy-racer look. The rear wing, which is standard on the GT, is a no-cost delete option. Both the V-6 and GT dispense with chrome accents around the windows, giving this retro shape a modern feel.

## A BIGGER FOOTPRINT

In fashioning this new take on a classic, Ford has a lot to work with. The new Mustang has a larger footprint than the model it replaces. It rides on a 107.1-inch wheelbase, up 5.8 inches, while overall length has grown 4.4 inches to 183.2. The 2005 Mustang is slightly wider at 73.9 inches (up from 73.1) and 1.4 inches taller at 54.5 inches.

This bigger package enables the Mustang to have a significantly wider track with 62.3 inches between the front wheels and 62.5 inches in the rear, up from the 59.9/60.1-inch front/rear stance of the previous model.

*The GT's dash is straightforward in execution. In addition to large vents and analog gauges, the center stack features easy-to-use climate controls and a 500-watt stereo or optional 1,000-watt system.*

*The chrome ball shifter for the five-speed manual seen in earlier prototypes has given way to this combination leather and aluminum knob.*

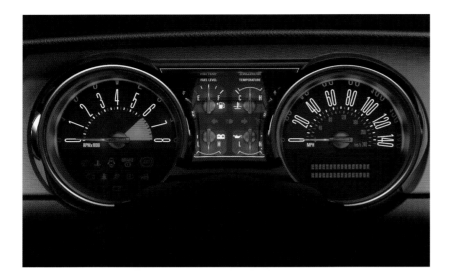

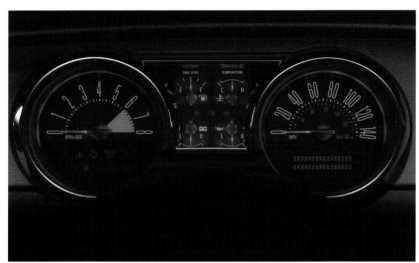

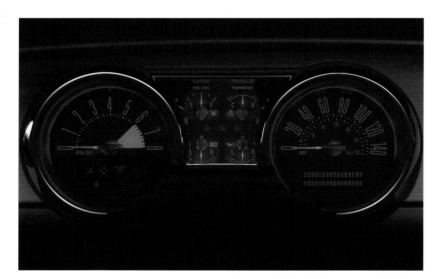

*A slick feature on the instrument cluster is adjustable lighting that allows the driver the option of picking one of 125 different shades ranging from pure white to purple.*

More space means a more spacious cabin. The Mustang is improved in nearly every measurement. Front headroom increases 1/2 inch to 38.6 inches, while legroom is up marginally from 42.6 to 42.7 inches. Hip room is increased in front by 1.3 inches to 53.6 inches and shoulder room grows nearly 2 inches from 53.6 to 55.4 inches.

The faster angle of the rear window on the new car compromises rear headroom slightly, which is down 1/2 inch to 35 inches, and rear hip room is down from 47.4 to 46.7 inches. Rear legroom is up 1/10 inch to 30.0 inches and shoulder room improved 1 inch to 53.3 inches.

Overall EPA (Environmental Protection Agency) volume for the passenger cabin is 96 cubic feet. Big gains have been made in trunk space, where the cargo capacity has been increased 13 percent, from 10.9 cubic feet to 12.3 cubic feet. The gas tank carries 16 gallons of fuel.

Inside, the cabin has an airy feel, thanks to the extra light let in by the rear quarter windows. Although the car is taller and has a slightly taller beltline than the previous model, the seating position is also higher, giving the driver a commanding view forward. The twin cockpit look is retained, but the rounded shapes of the 2004 Mustang have been supplanted by an angular twin-binnacle look that recalls the original model. The cowl is higher and more horizontal. An aluminum panel, standard on the GT and optional on the V-6, runs door-to-door and dominates the dash.

Base model V-6s without the aluminum dash panel are still smart looking. The black plastic dash is made of high-quality grained material and shows well against the standard chrome and aluminum accents around the instruments, vents, and door pulls.

Four large, chrome-ringed vents—two outboard and two above the center stack—are prominent details. The chrome-ringed instrument cluster features two main gauges: the tachometer on the left side and the speedometer on the right. A center section houses the gas gauge, water temperature, oil pressure, and volt readouts as well as warning lights and digital readouts for the trip computer and odometer.

With the turn of a rheostat, the driver can change the color of the background lighting of the instruments to one of 125 different shades, ranging from white to purple. The cluster is lit by three light-emitting diodes (LEDs) in base colors of red, green, and blue. Engineers control the brightness of the LED light by controlling the frequency with which each light is turned on and off. If the blue light is turned on and off faster than the red or green LEDs, more blue comes through to your eye. The light from these three LEDs is fed into acrylic light pipes where the colors are mixed into six pre-defined colors: white, blue, green, red, orange, and purple. The control knob allows the driver to blend these colors to a customized shade.

The steering wheel has a thick, grippy rim covered in leather, while a large round center hub houses the driver's airbag. The three-spoke wheel is dressed up with aluminum accents, and switches for the cruise control are mounted on two horizontal spokes. Turn signals and windshield wiper controls are stalk mounted, while the headlamps have a dash-mounted switch. The Mustang uses a conventional column-mounted key ignition.

The lower half of the dash and center stack have a matte black finish. Switches for the trip computer and traction control are mounted at the top and flank a single power point. The radio is positioned just below, and three levels of sound system are offered, starting with a base

*The V-6 Mustang presents a cleaner and leaner face to the world since it dispenses with the driving lights and the lower inlet is divided by just two bars to the GT's three.*

*The rear badge is yet another retro cue that echoes the simple Ford lettering of the 1960s and features the trademark galloping pony against a red, white, and blue backdrop.*

80-watt AM/FM stereo with CD player, a 500-watt step-up system with in-dash six-CD changer and MP3 capability, and a top-of-the line 1,000-watt premium audio system with six-CD changer. The 1,000-watt system is also equipped with trunk-mounted dual 500-watt subwoofers.

The climate controls have three simple dials: one for fan speed, another for temperature, and a third to direct the air. The console-mounted shifter for the five-speed manual was originally planned as a chrome ball, but early prototypes did not have a quality feel. The design was scrapped in favor of a leather-wrapped aluminum knob (originally developed for the European Mondeo) which has a higher quality appearance and warmer feel. The shifter for the automatic is a work of art in its own right. A chrome bezel surrounds the base, while the shift gate is made of brushed aluminum. The shift lever is also made of aluminum and resembles a jet aircraft throttle with a detent button on the left side and the lockout for overdrive on the right. On V-6 models without the aluminum dash, the automatic shifter is done up in a soft-touch matte black finish.

The center console is equipped with a hand brake, two large cup holders, and a covered bin that acts as an armrest between the front bucket seats. Like the center

stack, the console has a matte black finish. In addition to the center console bin, there are two map pockets in the doors and a glove box that takes up the lower half of the passenger side dash.

The front bucket seats (standard cloth on the V-6, leather on the GT) can be ordered in colors that either match or contrast with the interior. Contrasting seats in the GT are available in a solid color or with contrasting inserts. The vertical bar sew pattern on the seats also recall the original Mustang's interior.

The front buckets are comfortable and have noticeably more side and lower cushion bolstering than the previous model. The seats feature power adjustments for fore and aft positioning and height. The rake of the seatback is adjusted by a manual release. Small levers that

release the seatbacks are mounted high on the back of the front buckets for easy rear seat access. The lever has a memory function that repositions the seatback to the original rake.

In addition to more rear leg and shoulder room, the rear seats now have a standard 60/40-split fold-down feature that provides additional flexibility to the Mustang's load carrying capability. The seats themselves are more sculpted than the previous model to increase passenger comfort and support.

Standard features on all Mustangs include cruise control, air conditioning, power windows and door locks, and power outside mirrors. The sophisticated anti-theft system includes an alarm separate from the horn since many thieves look to disable the horn to defeat the anti-

theft system. There is an anti-tow sensor that detects when the front or the rear of the car is lifted and sounds the alarm and flashes the lights. The system also senses if a corner of the car has been jacked up to guard against wheel theft. Inside the car, an ultrasonic motion detector warns against "smash and grab" break-ins or when someone has put a hand or other object inside the car. Other sensors detect if a door or hood is opened and will sound an alarm.

## DRIVING THE GT

Once you slip behind the wheel of the 2005 Mustang GT, there's no mistaking the fact that the car is totally new. The larger passenger compartment is striking. The driver is not as closely coupled to the passenger; there's more

*The clean look of the V-6 carries around to the rear of the vehicle. On the base model there is no deck lid spoiler and just a single, discreet cutout for the exhaust pipe on the rear fascia.*

*The V-6 is pictured with a much more subdued color scheme and yet the choice of materials and graining gives the cockpit an upscale aura.*

*Base V-6 models are equipped with 16-inch 10-spoke alloy wheels with optional simulated knock-off hubs. Note the Ford blue oval in the center caps.*

elbow room, both in the center console area and in the space between the door and the front bucket.

The dashboard, in particular, signals change, not just because of its new design, but also the way it is positioned—flatter and further away than in the previous model. The cowl and beltline are higher, yet visibility remains good as the seating position, or H-point, has been raised slightly. With the push of a few buttons and a pull on the lever that controls rake it's easy for the driver to find a comfortable seating position. Thanks to the tilt steering, which has a lever on the left side of the steering column, the gauges are easily seen through the three-spoke steering wheel.

Turn the key and the GT's V-8 roars to life with a satisfying rumble. The Tremec T3650 five-speed manual has a much shorter gearshift lever than the previous Mustang. The stubby lever, coupled with short throws, gives the manual a very precise, almost hair-trigger, feel that allows you to snap off shifts with remarkable ease.

The clutch has a positive feel with just the right weighting to match up with the ease of the shifter. The

electronically controlled throttle is sprung to feel like a conventional throttle and provides the ability to precisely modulate engine output.

Of course, the first thing you have to do with the Mustang's 300 horsepower and 315 ft-lb of torque is drop the clutch and do a smoky burnout. The traction control is programmed to allow enough slip when the car is pointed forward on dry pavement to squeal the rear tires and let off a satisfying puff of tire smoke. If the car begins to slew, or it hits a patch of slippery terrain, the traction control quickly engages to rein the Mustang back in line. The combination of quick ABS sensors and the electronic throttle allows instantaneous reaction to excessive wheel slip. The system can be disabled by a dash-mounted switch.

The final drive on manual-equipped Mustangs is a 3.55:1 ring-and-pinion gear that provides snappy off-the-line acceleration. Ford expects 0–60 acceleration in the neighborhood of 5.5-seconds, while top speed is electronically limited at 143 miles per hour. The 8.8-inch

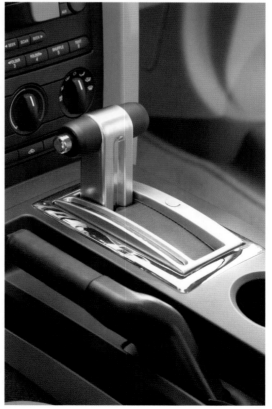

*Although there are fewer switches on the dash of the V-6, the controls are logically laid out and simple to use. The aluminum accent on the dash is an optional feature.*

*The shifter for the five-speed automatic has the look and feel of machined aluminum. A jet aircraft throttle inspired its shape.*

**111**

rear differential includes standard traction lock to provide better grip and smooth launches.

The automatic gives a bit away to the manual in terms of performance. Its extra 50 pounds bring curb weight up to 3,500 pounds; the automatic is equipped with a 3.31:1 final drive. The car's 0–60 acceleration is estimated to take about a half second longer. Still, the 5R55S transmission shifts seamlessly, due in large part to the electronic control system that communicates directly with the car's electronic throttle control system. In a refreshing change from trends, the automatic stays away from a manual sequential shift mode and relies on a

simple PRNDL arrangement for gear selection.

After a couple of traction control on and off burnouts we headed for the 1.5-mile handling course at Ford's Dearborn Proving Grounds. The track, with its series of increasing and decreasing radius turns, provides ample opportunity to test the dynamics of the 2005 Mustang GT.

The first thing you notice, even at low speeds, is the precision of the rack-and-pinion steering. It has a solid, linear feel to its action, due in part to the fact that its steering boost is fixed, not variable. As a result, the steering feel remains constant throughout its range of

motion, no matter the speed of the car. While this may require a bit more effort in parking maneuvers, the payoff comes in more precise and predictable steering at traveling speeds. You never feel a step-up in effort, (the hallmark of variable assist systems) which can lead to sloppy feedback from the steering. The Mustang's steering has excellent on-center feel; there's no dead spot at dead center and the car responds well when the wheel is moved off center.

Although the car retains a traditional solid rear axle, the new three-link setup, with a 1.5-inch-diameter Panhard rod, gives the car a settled feel. In cornering, the Mustang sticks well and provides a progressive feel as the suspension reaches its limits. The GT's 22-mm solid rear stabilizer bar adds to the solid feel of the rear end on the pavement. The previous-generation Mustang employed a four-bar link that didn't do a good a job in locating the rear axle. As a result, in hard cornering the rear always felt a little nervous and was quick in its transition from understeer to oversteer.

At the front, the independent MacPherson strut suspension, with reverse lower L-arm, feels much more solid and provides crisper turn-in than the previous model. The longer wheelbase and specially-tuned front

*The shark-nose styling of the Mustang adds to the impression of speed once the car is underway.*

bushings help smooth out the Mustang's ride without sacrificing the crisp feel of the handling.

Mark Rushbrook, Mustang's vehicle development manager, says much of the development of the GT centered on making the car as neutral as possible. "The GT had to be something that is very rewarding to drive, even rewarding when you go over the limit. We didn't want the car to go into terminal understeer. We wanted to make it very communicative so that you could feel the limits through the steering wheel and you could get the car back to where you want it not just with the steering wheel, but with the accelerator pedal and the brake pedal as well."

Chief engineer Thai-Tang says his experience in Europe convinced him that the car should be more neutral. "One of the things you learn in Europe, especially on the 'B' roads in the United Kingdom, is that when you get into a terminal understeer condition, it's very dangerous," he says. "You run into oncoming traffic. You have no maneuverability. So we've really tried to make this car more neutral and if you go into a corner

*The wider stance and revised three-link solid axle with Panhard rod keeps the Mustang firmly planted to the pavement in spirited driving.*

hot and start running into oncoming traffic, as soon as you get off the gas, the nose tucks in."

The suspension does exhibit a touch of understeer, a condition that can be driven through with judicious application of the throttle. Earlier prototypes exhibited a tendency to have more understeer and fairly quick roll gain. Although body lean is not excessive, the rate at which the car would pitch over and take a set was deemed to be a touch too high. Subsequent tuning of the shocks and bushings have slowed this rate down, giving the car's lateral motion a much more natural and progressive feel as it enters a corner.

Thai-Tang explains this roll change rate is related to the car's yaw center. "One of the things we find that

customers are real sensitive to is where the yaw center is. There are two extremes—one would be like a school bus, where the yaw center is way behind the vehicle and it feels as if it won't turn at all," he says. "The other is a rally car, where the yaw center is out in front of you and the rear end of the car is sliding all around." The early Mustang development mules had a yaw centerthat was somewhere in the trunk. As a result, the Mustang felt like a car that was much larger and as a result, less responsive. By retuning the shocks and stabilizing bars, the engineers were able to move the yaw center forward to right behind the front seats, giving the Mustang a much livelier feel.

*The clean lines of the design match the Mustang's handling—straightforward, predictable, and easy to drive.*

The car's nimbleness is complimented by the V-8 engine's tremendous flexibility, especially in the way the 315 ft-lb of torque is delivered. On the tight 1.5-mile handling loop, both second and third gear are effective, and even in some of the low-speed areas, the car pulls nicely in fourth gear. This seamless application of power enables the car to be very civil in low-speed operation, while at the same time possessing enough muscle to inspire confidence in 50–70 mile-per-hour passing maneuvers on two-lane blacktops.

The Mustang GT has 17x8-inch wheels shod with Pirelli P235/55 Z-rated rubber. The large contact patch and stiff, low-profile sidewalls give the GT plenty of grip to handle the V-8's output. Larger 18-inch wheels with BFGoodrich performance tires are also an option.

"On both cars, with respect to tire turning, we did trade off ultimate grip a little to get more progressive breakaway," Thai-Tang reveals. "We looked at tire submissions that had more overall grip, but once they break away, they were gone and there was nothing you could do about it. We dialed back on that a bit, to be a very flat curve right at the limit. As the tire starts to flag, you know what's happening, then you can steer it with the wheel, with the throttle, or with the brake to regain control."

In addition, the 2005 Mustang's better weight distribution and new suspension geometry with better camber have resulted in improved tire life.

The GT's brakes are exceptional. The front is equipped with 43-mm twin-piston calipers that grip 12.4-inch vented discs. The floating caliper is made of aluminum. At the rear, single-pot (also 43 mm) iron calipers grab 11.8-inch vented discs. The brake pedal has a firm feel with a high level of feedback that allows precise modulation of the brakes. The anti-lock system engages smoothly, slightly pulsing the pedal to let you know the ABS is engaged.

Even with its front-engine rear-drive layout, the Mustang doesn't feel nose heavy. The car's 54/46 front-to-rear weight distribution gives the Mustang a balanced feel. The car demands to be driven hard when the road begins to bend. Even though the suspension is not what one

would consider high-tech, its execution is clearly world-class and gives the GT solid, predictable, and above all enjoyable road manners, whether you're out for a Sunday drive or caught in the slog of a daily commute.

The attention paid to the body structure has a tremendous payoff in the solid feel of the Mustang.

There's no noticeable body flex in cornering, and there are no rattles or creaks as on the previous car.

"There is a big jump in refinement," Thai-Tang proudly points out. "That's everything from craftsmanship, fit and finish, use of higher quality materials, right down to sound qualities and the elimination of all the error

states, such as buzzes, vibrations, squeaks and rattles, wind noise, and clunks in the drivetrain."

There is no looseness or lash in the body or drivetrain. Fits and gaps are tight and there is little in the way of drivetrain vibration transmitted into the cockpit. The stiffness of the body translates directly into the

*Even without the large inboard driving lights, the V-6 is instantly recognizable as a Mustang.*

surefooted feel of the car on the handling course. And while the V-8's music is unmistakable, unwanted road and wind noise are filtered out. The Mustang is a delightful companion for tackling a challenging track or taking a cross-country jaunt.

Most enjoyable of all, though, is the exhaust note. Thai-Tang says the engineers worked especially hard to get the sound right.

"In the old car, we had the mufflers ahead of the axle," he explains. "From a sound-imaging standpoint, it was much closer to the driver, and then from a musical instrument point of view, the longer exhaust pipe was easier to tune. Now we have rear mufflers behind the axles with a short pipe. The team has done a great job of still getting that very muscular, signature sound, which was much more difficult with the new architecture."

The GT has a throaty exhaust rumble that rekindles all the warm and fuzzy memories of the late 1960s and early 1970s American muscle car era. There's nothing more satisfying than the bass drum beat of eight cylinders thrumming in unison. That rumble quickly transforms into an angry snarl when the accelerator is mashed to the floor. Combined with the shriek of smoking tires, the words set to this music would most certainly be, "Let the good times roll."

## WHEN LESS IS MORE

In the V-6 coupe version, the Mustang may not look as aggressive as its GT stablemate, but that doesn't mean it isn't an engaging car to drive. Compared to the previous V-6 Mustang, this new model is not only more refined, but also offers greater performance and a bolder exhaust note to match.

Barb Samardzich, Ford's executive director of small front- and rear-wheel-drive vehicles, explains, "The majority of V-6 customers are women over 30. They're looking for something that is their day-to-day transportation. This car has to have a reasonable level of refinement as well as be a fun sports car. They want that sportiness, but they don't want one that is going to beat them up day in and day out, or make trade-offs that sacrifice ride."

According to Thai-Tang, the overriding philosophy in developing the V-6 was to make a car that could stand on

*With an optional rear spoiler and graphics, this V-6 looks tough like the GT without losing its simplicity.*

its own merits. "We don't want the V-6 customers to feel like they are settling for less. All Mustang customers buy into the image of the classic American muscle car. Seventy percent of all Mustang buyers buy the V-6 and the majority of them are women and youth buyers who go into the V-6 primarily due to affordability. But what we've done is to make it very accessible. We've dialed back on the boy racer part of it to make it a much more livable car. But at the same time, we don't want them to feel like they are settling for less."

While the V-6 doesn't have quite the same visual punch as the GT, it is a far cry from the secretaries' car of the original Mustang. Those cars, most often notchbacks, had chrome brightwork and vinyl tops. The

pounds for the manual and 3,345 for the automatic. Considering that the 2005 V-6 is larger and more powerful than its predecessor, the fact that its base curb weight is up only 10 pounds is a credit to Ford engineering.

The V-6 coupe delivers its power through a 3.31:1 final drive, so it doesn't have the snappiness of the GT, but it's a big improvement over the previous model, which had a 3.27:1 final drive and 193 horsepower. Ford estimates 0–60 acceleration of the V-6 manual at about 7 seconds and 7.5 seconds for the five-speed automatic.

With slightly less weight on the nose than the GT, the V-6, which has a 53/47 percent front/rear weight distribution, feels nimble and spirited in cornering. The 15.7:1 steering ratio remains the same for both cars, but the taller profile P215/65 S-rated tires on 16x7-inch alloys don't offer the same level of grip as the larger wheel and tire package on the GT. Turn-in is just as crisp, but at the limits the V-6 tends to push a bit more and steps out in the rear sooner than the GT. This is also due in part to the rear suspension, which doesn't benefit from a stabilizer bar. The front bar, partially because of the lighter nose, is only 28.6 mm in diameter as opposed to the GT's 34-mm front bar.

"On the V-6, we were willing to give up a little more grip for ride comfort," Vehicle Development Manager Rushbrook says. "We wanted to make sure that it was very safe at the limit. You will get some more understeer if you drive too aggressively and go over the limit."

While there is noticeably more push in the V-6, the car's attitude can still be adjusted with throttle inputs. It feels much more neutral than the previous Mustang, but less so than the GT. The payoff shows on the high-speed oval at Ford's Dearborn Proving Grounds, where the V-6 has a suppler ride and is less prone to hopping over tar strips and expansion joints.

The steering system is the same as the GT, with the same boost curve, T-bar, and gearing. When pressed hard, the taller profile tires on the V-6 model provide more feedback through the steering, making the action seem a little less responsive and tighter than the GT's steering.

*The black rocker panel and taller profile 16-inch tires gives the Mustang V-6 the appearance of a higher ride height than the GT.*

shape said sporty, while the equipment on board delivered economy.

The V-6 delivers economy car mileage, but it's no slouch in the performance department. Rated at 210 horsepower at 5,250 rpm and 240 ft-lb of torque at 3,500 rpm, the 4.0-liter V-6 packs tremendous punch when you take into account that the car tips the scales at 3,300

The five-speed automatic is a fine match for the 4.0-liter V-6. By adding an extra gear to the transmission (the previous Mustang had a four-speed automatic), engineers were able to use closer and lower ratios to improve acceleration. That the five-speed automatic readily communicates with the electronic throttle control is most apparent when the car is floored from a standing start. The shifts are immediate with little drop-off in rpm. In particular, the second to third upshift occurs without the tachometer

falling below 5,000 rpm, ensuring that the engine remains in the fat parts of the torque and power curves when maximum performance is most needed. And in steady-state cruising, the electronic controls provide nearly instantaneous gear kickdown when the throttle is mashed to the floor.

Thai-Tang believes a real "sleeper" in the Mustang line will be the V-6 equipped with the five-speed manual. "The V-6 manual is also a really nice package as far as performance feel," Thai-Tang notes. "The transmission's

*With less weight on the nose, the Mustang V-6's handling has a lively, nimble feel.*

*Tuned for a suppler ride and more understeer, the Mustang V-6 is designed to appeal to sporty car buyers who depend on their cars for daily transportation.*

internals have been changed with more precise machining of the gear set to provide smoother operation." When equipped with this upgraded Tremec T-5 five-speed manual (ironically, the internals are the same ones that were previously used on the Chevy Camaro), the V-6 can be a hoot to drive. It's fairly quick and predictable like its GT sibling.

Because the V-6 has less mass and is electronically limited to a top speed of 112 miles per hour, the front brakes aren't quite as large as those on the GT. The front discs are 11.5 inches in diameter, while the rear setup is the same as the GT, with 11.8-inch rotors.

Like the GT, particular attention was paid to the sound coming from the exhaust. Although the V-6 is designed to appeal to a more female and younger audience, it was felt that the exhaust note should be deeper and slightly more aggressive to reflect the changes beneath the hood. As a result, there's a bit more bark and rasp to the exhaust. It's interesting to note that the single exhaust proved to be a bigger challenge in exhaust note tuning. It was the V-6, and not the GT, that exceeded pass-by noise standards in initial testing. This note in early

prototypes was dialed back significantly in subsequent test rides. Thai-Tang notes that with just one exhaust and 4.0 liters of displacement, the V-6 is pushing much more air (which makes noise) through the exhaust than the V-8's dual exhaust, making it a bigger challenge to get the sound right.

The increased performance, new look, and sound of the V-6 are expected to broaden the car's appeal to younger male buyers who may not be able to afford the GT, or more importantly, the insurance on a V-8 sports car.

The V-6 offers the option to dress it up like a GT, thanks to the rear spoiler and other Mustang graphics, or to spec it out as a clean, modern coupe that is smart looking and simple in its design. Either way, there's enough performance under the hood and in the suspension to satisfy the most demanding of buyers. And to think the sticker starts at less than $20,000.

"The V-6 is much more fun to drive than the previous version," Samardzich stresses. "After getting our management team through it, they were surprised and delighted by the performance of the V-6. The performance feel is terrific and we over-achieved our objectives for the car."

*The 60/40-split fold-down rear seat has ample pass-through to the trunk, greatly increasing the flexibility of the Mustang's load carrying capability.*

# Seven

# The SVT Connection

## Past and Future SVT Cobras

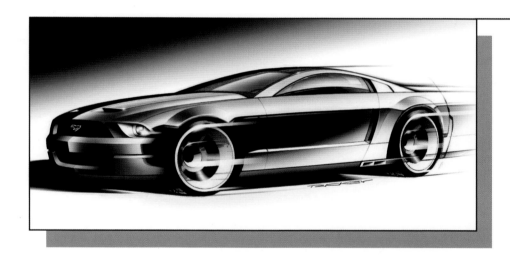

"Every successive improvement requires a big step up in power. We're going to have to bring in another 80 to 90 horsepower to be sure there is no question that this car is a lot faster than the old model.

—O. John Coletti,
*Ford manager of business planning*

*Ford's Special Vehicle Team traces its roots to the 1984 Mustang SVO, which used a turbocharged 2.3-liter four-cylinder engine to produce the same output as a V-8. Unfortunately, the vehicle's high price spelled its demise.*

NJECTING AN EXTRA ELEMENT OF PERFORMANCE INTO the Mustang has always been a part of the car's legacy. Going back to the 1960s, there were variants like the Shelby Mustang, Boss 302, and Mach 1. Carrying on that legacy today is the SVT Mustang Cobra. And as part of the new Mustang program, SVT promises there will again be another Cobra model . . . but not right away.

To understand how the Cobra variant fits in Ford's overall strategy for Mustang, a little history is in order.

BMW pioneered the concept of factory-tuned, high-output, limited-production cars with BMW Motorsports' M-series cars. Ford took some fledgling steps to mimic BMW's success in the 1980s by establishing its Special Vehicle Operations (SVO) as a source of aftermarket performance and racing parts, using it as a springboard to build a factory-tuned Mustang.

That first effort was the European-inspired SVO Mustang, which debuted in 1984. While the stock Mustang GT still retained its pushrod V-8 and rather straightforward approach to the pony car genre, the SVO Mustang was envisioned as a technological tour de force that would rival the best that Europe had to offer. A 2.3-liter turbocharged and intercooled inline four was used. The sophisticated suspension used gas-charged shocks,

revised spring settings, and large low-profile tires to improve the handling. The exterior sported aerodynamic body cladding and a bi-plane rear spoiler that contributed to its European looks.

The car was a technical marvel and a marketing disaster. Priced nearly $6,000 more than the GT, both cars were rated at 145 horsepower. Even though engine power was eventually moved up to 200 horsepower, the SVO Mustang never sold as well as the V-8 GT and was dropped after the 1986 model year after only 9,844 were sold. SVO reverted to its original charter of supplying racing and performance parts to the aftermarket.

The idea of a special Mustang performance model lay fallow for several years until Neil Ressler, executive director of vehicle engineering, decided to revisit the issue in 1990. According to Jim Campisano's official SVT history, *Powered by SVT, Celebrating a Decade of Ford Performance*, Ressler asked Janine Bay, an engineer working in planning and strategy, to come up with a higher performance version of the Mustang 5.0 HO using SVO racing parts. Bay found that a set of GT40 heads from the catalog boosted the output of the Mustang's 5.0 HO by 40 horsepower. The prototype was called the Mustang GT40.

*The same year the Mustang Cobra bowed, SVT introduced a limited run of 107 Mustang Cobra R models, stripped down and pumped specifically for club racing.*

*Along with the stock SN95 Mustangs for 1994, SVT launched its replacement for the Cobra based on the Fox-4 platform. This model produced 240 horsepower, up slightly over the '93 model.*

The car was shown at an executive review attended by Robert Rewey, Ford Division executive vice president of sales and marketing. It was a car Rewey had been waiting for. Earlier in his career at Lincoln-Mercury, Rewey had put together Lincoln-Mercury's own line of European-inspired performance cars called the Merkur. Working with Rewey

*The revamped Mustang Cobra was offered in both coupe and convertible for the first time, with the ragtop receiving the honor of pacing the 1994 Indianapolis 500.*

Special Vehicle Engineering (SVE), headed by Janine Bay. Rewey set up the distribution and sales organization, which became known as Special Vehicle Team (SVT). John Plant was named specialty vehicle manager for this group.

By the time the Mustang GT40 was ready for release as a 1993 model, Ford's attorneys changed the name to Cobra, believing that if Ford didn't use the moniker it owned, it would slip into the public domain. The other SVT product in Ford's lineup that year was a performance-tuned version of the F-150 pickup called Lightning.

From the beginning, either by happenstance or intent, SVT had a history of timing many of its new product launches at the end of a product's lifecycle. The 1993 Mustang Cobra debuted during the last model year of the original Fox chassis. Not as aggressive looking as the GT, the '93 Cobra shared the same chin spoiler and fog lamps, but had a small grille opening sporting the galloping pony, something not seen on a Mustang in 15 years. Thanks to the GT40 heads and intake system, the Cobra produced 235 horsepower compared to the stock 5.0 HO's 205 horsepower. (In publishing those numbers, it was believed that Ford was being conservative because early tests with the GT40 prototype showed a 40

in establishing that division was John Plant, who also worked on the SVO Mustang and had an extensive background working in Europe and America for BMW, Opel, and Fiat.

When Ford Chairman Harold "Red" Poling signed off on the Mustang GT40 concept in 1991, Ressler formed

*In an effort to respond to the use of the Corvette 350-ci 275-horsepower LS-1 engine in Chevy's Camaro, SVT built a limited run of 1995 Mustang Cobra R models, powered by a 351-ci V-8 producing 300 horsepower. Like the first Cobra R, the '95 was stripped down for track duty. Only 250 were built.*

horsepower gain.) In addition to the extra horsepower under the hood, the Cobra's suspension took a different tack that stressed compliance and ride as much as good grip. That meant using softer springs from the four-cylinder Mustang in the rear as well as a smaller diameter sway bar up front. Wheels were larger 17-inch alloys and the tires featured an asymmetric unidirectional pattern. And the Cobra was the first Mustang since the SVO model to benefit from four-wheel disc brakes.

From the SVO experience, Ford learned that even though the Cobra was being pitched as a premium product, it could not be priced in the stratosphere. As a result, the car carried a sticker of $18,505, just $2,400 more than the stock GT.

## R IS FOR RACING

Meanwhile, Ford was looking to flex this newfound muscle on the track as well as the street. The company decided to offer the Mustang Cobra R, a special racing version of the street car, for use in SCCA and IMSA sanctioned events. The Cobra R was built on the regular Mustang assembly line using some pull-ahead pieces from the redesigned 1994 Mustang, including the lower control arms and five-bolt 17-inch wheels. Since weight is an issue in racing, the Cobra R was a bare-bones machine—no radio, air conditioning, rear seats, or carpeting. There were no power assists for the steering and the windows had hand cranks. By deleting all this equipment, 450 pounds were saved. The suspension

featured stiff Eibach springs, adjustable Koni shocks, and large 13-inch front and 11.65-inch rear vented disc brakes. Up front the Cobra R had a new radiator and oil and transmission coolers. The Cobra's 5.0-liter pushrod motor with the GT40 heads remained unchanged for the R model, as was the Borg Warner T5 manual transmission. The rarest of all SVT products, only 107 of the '93 Cobra R model, costing just over $25,000 per copy, were built.

When the revamped SN95 debuted in 1994, SVT expanded the Cobra line to include both the coupe and convertible. In addition to sharing the SN95's new bodywork, the Cobra was fitted with new front and rear fascias, its own deck lid and spoiler, and inside a new

gauge cluster with white-faced instruments, as well as magnesium seat frames for the front buckets.

The lessons learned from the more compliant '93 model were applied to the '94. Linear rate 400 lb/in front and 160 lb/in rear springs replaced the variable rate coils. The stiffer front springs were offset by a smaller-than-stock front roll bar, while in the rear, a slightly larger sway bar better controlled body roll and reduced understeer. And again, a 17-inch wheel and tire package was specified with grippy Goodyear GS-C rubber. The GT40 V-8 was carried over with horsepower bumped to 240 and torque increased to 285 ft-lb, though it was still less than the 275 horsepower Camaro and Firebird models produced with the detuned Corvette LS1 powerplant.

*Although the exterior remained the same, the 1996 model saw its stalwart 5.0-liter pushrod V-8 replaced by a 305-horsepower 4.6-liter dual overhead cam V-8 from Ford's Modular engine family.*

*Along with the body style change in 1999, the SVT Mustang Cobra received significant chassis improvements, including the addition of an independent rear suspension for the first time.*

The Cobra was chosen as the pace car for the 1994 Indianapolis 500, and 1,000 pace car replicas were built that year. The following year, the Cobra convertible was the only Mustang offered with a removable hardtop, an option originally promised across the board but later abandoned and limited to the 1995 model year run of Cobras.

Also in 1995, SVT resurrected the Cobra R. Special Vehicle Engineering, which had been passed from Janine Bay to Rod Mansfield of Ford's European operation, was now given to O. John Coletti, who was manager of business planning on the SN95 project that saved the Mustang.

Coletti was looking for a way to respond to the LS1-powered Camaros and Firebirds on the track. "How do you answer a 350-cubic-inch Camaro, but with a 351-cubic-inch Mustang?" Coletti says. That engine was a marine version of the Windsor V-8 and again used the GT40 heads and revised intake manifold, which gave the car an honest 300 horsepower and 365 ft-lb of torque.

*The SVT tradition of producing R models continued with the limited-run 2000 Cobra R. This time, a 5.4-liter DOHC V-8, the one found in the Lincoln Navigator, was wedged into the engine compartment and with its specially tuned intake manifold, pumped out 385 horsepower.*

Like the first Cobra R, the '95 model lacked air conditioning, radio, rear seat, carpeting, and sound-deadening insulation. The hood was fiberglass, not necessarily for weight saving, but more for the clearance of the taller 351 V-8. The car's stock 15.4-gallon gas tank was replaced by a 20-gallon fuel cell, which underscored the Cobra R's racing pedigree, as did the stiffer progressive springs and adjustable Koni shocks. Only 250 of the $35,000 1995 Cobra R models were built.

In 1996, the venerable pushrod 5.0-liter V-8 was dropped from the lineup in favor of the new generation 4.6-liter overhead cam Modular V-8. While stock horsepower remained at 215 horsepower in the GT, despite the drop in displacement, SVT delivered more power by going with a four-valve dual overhead cam version of the 4.6 found in the Mark VIII.

By designing its own dual-stage, equal-length intake manifold, SVT was able to increase the output of the engine to 305 horsepower and 300 ft-lb of torque. To announce the presence of this new muscular motor, a new hood was designed with a power bulge and dual intake nostrils. The three-bar vertical taillamp treatment, a Mustang tradition, reappeared on all '96 Mustangs and Cobras. Packing the additional punch, Ford claimed 0-to-60-mile-per-hour acceleration of 5.9 seconds and a quarter-mile time of 13.99 at 101.6 miles per hour.

By the time the 1999 redesign of the Mustang came around, the SVT was an integral part of Ford's marketing program for the car. After six years of promoting the SVT brand and establishing a specific dealer network, the SVT Mustang Cobra had developed into the performance flagship for the division's car line.

According to Coletti, up until 1999, the Cobra had been about raw power, trying to match GM's F-cars pony for pony. But the addition of the smooth-revving overhead cam 4.6-liter V-8 brought a new level of refinement to the Mustang that had been lacking since the Euro-inspired SVO days of the early 1980s. Rather than looking for a significant increase in output, SVT tackled the task of creating a Cobra that would have the handling and refined road manners of a sporting European machine, adding a new dimension to a class of cars that had relied primarily on drag strip, solid axle launches for thrills.

In Campisano's history of SVT, Janine Bay, who was in charge of the Mustang program in 1999, stated, "With its new independent rear suspension, the SVT Cobra breaks away from other pony cars in this segment—a

*Fitted with an Eaton Roots-type supercharger, the 4.6-liter engine uses intercooling to produce as much torque (390 ft-lb) as it does horsepower.*

segment named for the first Mustang. The ride and handling characteristics Cobra offers are world-class in every respect."

More than that, the team's approach to bringing an independent rear suspension to Mustang was as innovative as it was daring. While the rest of the Mustang lineup would retain its solid axle, the new independent rear would be designed and built as a modular unit to be

bolted in the same space on the same assembly line as the regular cars. In essence, the setup would be reverse-engineered from the mounting points of the solid rear axle.

In addition to the independent rear suspension which, true to Cobra tradition offered better grip and a suppler ride than the GT, was another increase in power, this time to 320 horsepower. But unlike the original '93 model, which was renowned for being stouter than its

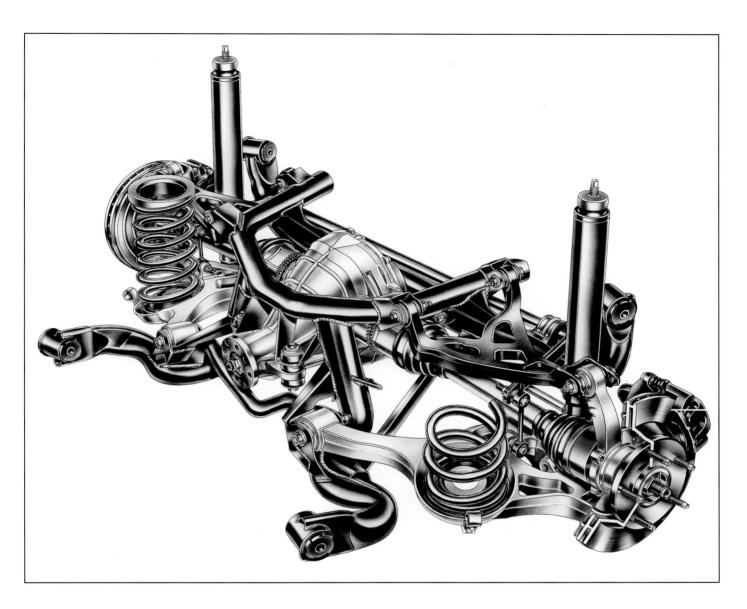

235 horsepower, some Cobras came up short of the advertised horsepower. A crash program to find a fix resulted in new intake manifold components and a less restrictive exhaust system offered to '99 Cobra owners. This derailed plans for a 2000 model year Mustang Cobra.

But it didn't stop SVT from producing another R model. The 2000 Cobra R followed the formula laid down by the previous two versions: a stripped-down body, race-bred suspension (this time one that could take advantage of an independent rear) and, of course, big horsepower. To do this, Coletti's team reworked Ford's Triton 5.4-liter V-8. Sitting atop the engine was a specially tuned intake manifold with short trumpets feeding four-valve heads similar to those used by Ford's Rough Riders off-road

truck racing team. The exhaust manifolds fed a Bassani X pipe and Borla dual exhaust that exited on the left side of the car, just ahead of the rear wheels. The engine, which produced 385 horsepower and 385 ft-lb of torque, was fitted with catalytic converters, making it a street-legal racing car.

The look of the Cobra R was intimidating, thanks to a huge front air dam (it was shipped in the trunk for dealer installation), 18-inch wheels, and a tall rear wing. Inside, the Cobra R had Recaro sports seats, a Tremec T56 six-speed gearbox, and little else in the way of creature comforts or sound insulation.

Coletti says that while only 300 of the 2000 Cobra R models were sold (at an astounding MSRP of $55,000),

*SVT prides itself on developing a modular independent rear suspension that bolts up into the same space as the solid rear axle. This operation is done on the same assembly line as the GT and V-6 models and will continue with the next generation Mustang Cobra.*

the project provided some keen insights into the future of the Mustang Cobra for its last go-around on the SN95 platform and for the future SVT Cobra that will come from the all-new Mustang.

The first insight was in the area of refinement. "What surprised me about the Cobra R was how easy it was to drive on the street, but also how much refinement it lacked because we threw away the insulation, the radio, and the air conditioning," Coletti recalls. "We had so much power and torque, I felt we didn't need to do away with all those creature comforts. What were we saving, 90 pounds? We could have done a much nicer street R if we wanted."

The second insight gained by the Cobra R was that if SVT wanted more performance out of its regular Mustang Cobra, it would have to either increase the displacement of the 4.6-liter V-8 or use forced induction. After resuming Mustang Cobra production for the 2001 model year, the car went on hiatus again for 2002 as the all-new 2003 model was being developed.

"We had one prototype of the 2003 Cobra that we took on an infamous trip out West that had a 340-horsepower normally aspirated 4.6-liter V-6," Coletti says. "It had more power than the stock motor, but we had to give up some torque to get the top end. At lower speeds it could not outrun the 2001 car. Sure, after a mile and a half you might catch the 2001 car and pass him, but that's not what our customer is all about. We had taken the naturally aspirated engine as far as it could go and decided that we needed to blow on the engine."

The prototype, known internally as the Terminator, used an Eaton Roots-type supercharger to take the 4.6-liter V-8's power from 320 to 390 horsepower and torque from 385 to 390 ft-lb. Coletti says the use of supercharging totally changed the equation.

"In 1993, the Cobra R would do the quarter mile in 13 seconds. When we did the 300 horsepower Cobra R in 1995, all of a sudden we're under 13. Then we came back with the 2000 Cobra R and dipped into the 12s. Now with the 2003 production Cobra, not the stripped-down R mind you, we're solidly in the 12s. Did we give up anything? No, not when you look at the fact that you get

air conditioning, a radio, good sound insulation. So if you look at the progression of the Cobra, it's really a 12-second car with all the amenities. That's pretty impressive. And you know what? In 2004 we don't pay the gas guzzler tax."

The 2003 SVT Mustang Cobra was worth the wait of an extra model year, not only for its smooth, powerful drivetrain, but also for its braking power (thanks to 13-inch front and 11.65-inch rear Brembos) and crisp

handling. In addition to being supercharged for the first time, the Mustang Cobra also received specific chassis tuning for coupe and convertible models. Although spring rates remained the same, the front stabilizer bar was increased by a millimeter to better control body roll, and Bilstein gas-charged monotube shocks replaced the twin tube units.

Other changes included a new hood profile with twin air exactors to accommodate the taller supercharged engine and new bolder front and rear fascias, including a rear bumper cover with the Cobra name embossed in large letters. The interior was spruced up with new leather seats sporting suede inserts, titanium-colored instrument faces, and a steering wheel with a thicker rim. But its launch during the waning days of the current Fox-4 platform meant that after the 2004 models were gone, there wouldn't be a replacement for at least two years.

*A hint of the next SVT Mustang Cobra R can be seen in the aggressive front end of the GT coupe concept presented at the 2003 North American International Auto Show. The wider grille and air scoops on the hood are reminiscent of the current car.*

## COLETTI ON THE NEXT COBRA

"So now the question is, what do we do with the next one?" Coletti asks. "Obviously, if you look at the progression of models in the past and connect the dots, guess where we're going? It's going to be packing a lot more horsepower than the old model."

Coletti notes that for every few tenths shaved off the quarter mile, the horsepower needed to achieve that goal rises exponentially. "Every successive improvement requires a big step up in power. So what does that tell you about the next car? We're going to have to bring in another 80 to 90 horsepower more to be sure there is no question that this car is a lot faster than the old model. Just to get two- or three-tenths out of it, you have to put down a lot more power. So you can expect a big power increase."

That power increase will come from both an increase in displacement and a switch from a Roots to screw-type supercharger. SVT, which developed the Ford GT, looked in that car's midship engine bay for the answer: a 5.4-liter V-8 with the screw-type supercharger that produces 500 horsepower. Look for a similar setup to produce somewhere in between that figure and the 2004 Mustang Cobra's 390 horsepower.

Even though the 2005 Mustang's platform is new, it still retains its solid axle layout. So SVT is busy working on a modular independent rear suspension for the Cobra, a similar approach to what was done on the last model.

"There was no way we were going to stick with the solid axle," Coletti says. "If we went back to a solid axle, we would be crucified. It's an admission of defeat—you can't do that."

With the new platform comes a totally new set of challenges in packaging a short- and long-arm independent rear in the same space as the new Mustang's solid rear axle. It represents the biggest engineering challenge in developing the new Cobra.

"It was tough," Coletti admits. "An IRS module is completely different than a solid axle in terms of clearance. The first thing you want is suspension travel; you would like to have plus/minus of 6 inches. IRS is in a completely different envelope when it comes to tire clearance and its range of motion as opposed to a wheel attached to solid axle. The independent wheel travels along more of an arc, while the wheel on a solid axle just moves up and down."

Then there's the challenge of working within the standard Mustang's frame rail and attachment points. "Here's where it gets complicated," Coletti says. "The rear axle envelope and sheet metal are already fixed. You have to package it in the existing subframe, and then you have to optimize the geometry of the travel, and then you have to isolate the subframe from the body because you don't want the thing buzzing the rear end. Because of the confined space, you have to overcome the lack of mechanical advantage for the links. Then you start to develop links that you've never seen before, strange-looking upper links. I would say that was the biggest challenge, although because of the step up in power and torque, we have also had a lot of work to do with the half-shafts and rear differential."

Coletti says the current six-speed manual will return, probably with a twin-disc clutch. But don't look for any Formula One–style paddle shifter or fancy stability control systems on the Cobra.

"A Mustang guy wants to use his foot and wants to be in control of the car," Coletti says. "My impression is I don't want to put anything between the driver and the car. This is the American muscle car psyche: 'I am the brains of this car, I am in control.' If you offer them the choice of all these transmissions like Formula One shifters, you know what they would want? More power."

There's a certain honesty in this approach of offering a straightforward muscle car that can handle. "In the products that we do, we like to use technology that is basically proven, reliable, and effective. All this novelty stuff—four-wheel steer, you name it—our customers don't want it. Yaw control, they don't want it. You can have traction control, but you better give them an off switch. They want good brakes and even better acceleration."

Coletti's goals for the car's performance are equally straightforward. "In the functional areas of straight-line acceleration, skid pad numbers, braking numbers, and road course numbers, the next Cobra has to be a clear winner over the old car."

Like the previous generation Cobras, the new car will share major body panels with the Mustang GT. Coletti promised differentiation in the car with the lighting treatments and bolt-on components, including hood, chin spoilers, rocker extensions, and rear wings. "If you look at the pattern over the years, we're not going too far away from it," Coletti explains. "We've touched the hood. We've done deck lid spoilers, taillight differences, and front and rear fascias. Generally we don't change sheet metal; I'd love to play with it, but on low-volume cars, it's expensive."

One area to expect differentiation from the standard Mustang line would be the interior. "We always spend a lot of money on the interior. In our world, if you have the fifty bucks, you put it right where the customer sees it. You upgrade the seats and touch points like the shifter, the parking brake handle, the steering wheel. Everything you want has to have a nice feel to it. We'll use perforated leather on the steering wheel and seats."

Of particular interest will be the instrument cluster. "We'll have a boost gauge and a higher reading speedometer," Coletti promises. In the past, SVT has gone with a white-faced gauge theme. "But now everyone is doing it, so we'll do something different. What we want is for the customers to feel and be constantly reminded that they have a Cobra."

Doug Gaffka, who started the Mustang design process with J Mays, is working on the new version of the SVT Mustang Cobra. Mays says the car will have the aggressiveness of the Mustang concepts, especially in the hood and grille area.

Coletti adds, "It's much more aggressive than the Mustang. It has larger wheels and tires, a wider stance. Not only do we want the front to be more aggressive, we want the rear to be highly differentiated, because most people will be seeing the car from the rear."

Coletti says another area that is being worked extensively is underhood appearance. "On the Cobra, everyone wants to look under the hood. We want to tie it all together and give it a nice look," he says. And true to the SVT Mustang Cobra heritage, there will be a convertible.

The big question is when? "We do our programs in 24-month cycles, so look for it in 2006, perhaps as an '07 model," Coletti hints. And beyond? "We have our hands full with Cobra now, but if we think of something really slick, we could do a new Cobra R to push the envelope." And so the beat goes on.

# Eight

# The Past as a Prelude

## What the Future Has in Store

The ability to change and adapt the Mustang to not only rekindle fond memories of the old car, but also to create new versions that will appeal to younger buyers with no sense of that history, is critical to long-term success.

*The GT-R concept works on many levels, demonstrating a future race car, while at the same time paying homage to Ford racing and design heritage.*

DECIPHERING WHAT'S NEXT FOR THE MUSTANG IS as simple as looking back at the rich history of this icon. What the Mustang has been, from simple six-cylinder pony car, to fire-breathing V-8 muscle car, is what the new car will be. Ironically, taking the overall design back to the car's early history has opened up a wide range of possibilities and variants. It promises a steady stream of cars that will carry names like Mach 1, Boss 302, and maybe even Shelby GT350, all of which will keep the new Mustang fresh for years to come.

The first step in this process of widening the car's appeal was the introduction of a convertible. Although Ford showed a convertible concept at the 2003 North American International Auto Show, it kept details of the production ragtop under tight wraps in order to make a splash with the car's introduction in spring 2005.

From the beginning of the Mustang's redesign, a convertible was a given in both V-6 and V-8 GT trim. As such, the car's structure was carefully developed to have the necessary strength and rigidity to accommodate a roofless design. In fact, the need for a ragtop drove many of the design elements common to both the coupe and convertible.

*Although the production convertible won't have a sport bar, the concept was clearly influenced by this 1968 Mustang GT500 KR convertible.*

Originally, Ford Group Vice President of Design J Mays envisioned Mustang coupes with a U-shaped backlight, a cue taken from the 1965 fastback. Instead, that rear window bottom had to be squared off so that the coupe and convertible could share the same stamping for the rear deck. Although both cars utilize common lower body panels, there are other changes that give the convertible a different feel than the coupe.

Even with the top up, the convertible has a personality all its own. The most obvious is that the soft top doesn't have the signature flying C-pillar with its quarter window. Instead there are two small power quarter windows that meet the side glass. The daylight opening is viewed as a single piece instead of two separate openings as on the coupe. In addition, the convertible top, when in place, is just a touch lower than the roofline of the coupe, giving the car a more sinister look, like a speedster or chopped hot rod. The top operation promises to be simple, with a manual latch release and a power fold-down mechanism. The Mustang's roof has a semi-hard front panel that gives the look of a tonneau cover when retracted. Much attention was paid to the stack height of the folded top so that it rests flush with the rear deck lid. Even with the additional bracing and the installation of the top and its power mechanism, the convertible is expected to weigh within 200 pounds of the coupe.

Long before the public caught a glimpse of the production version of the convertible, Ford decided to whet the appetite of hard-core enthusiasts about the possibilities this new Mustang will hold for the future.

*The star of the 2004 New York Auto Show was the Mustang GT-R concept. This show car not only marked the 40th anniversary of the Mustang's launch in high style, but also demonstrated that there is tremendous design and package flexibility in this new generation.*

*The GT-R and many of its graphic details were inspired by the Bud Moore Mustangs that won the 1970 Trans-Am championship. Here Parnelli Jones is at the wheel of this famous racer.*

April 2004 marked the 40th anniversary of the original Mustang's launch at the New York World's Fair. In honor of that event, Ford threw a little birthday bash for the Mustang in conjunction with the New York Auto Show.

### R IS FOR RACING, PART II

The centerpiece was the GT-R Mustang, a concept of a potential race car that paid homage to Ford's clinching of both the manufacturer and driver championships in the 1970 Trans-Am series. Painted Valencia Orange, the Mustang GT-R recalled the famous Bud Moore Mustangs campaigned by George Follmer and series champ Parnelli Jones.

Doug Gaffka, who worked on the production Mustang before moving over to head design for the Ford Performance Group, says the GT-R was a natural. "We decided that when a car as good as the 2005 Mustang comes along, we don't need to look much further for a pure race car."

Starting with the car's original shape, senior designer Keith Rogman and Gaffka reworked the front end with a design that recalls the nose of the original Trans-Am cars. Instead of stock round headlamps, a horizontal bar divides the openings with small projector beams positioned above and below. Pop rivets hold the large honeycomb grille in place with twin cooling fans easily seen through the pattern. The aggressiveness is carried over beneath the bumper line where a large lower air inlet flanked by additional driving lights sits atop a carbon fiber aerodynamic splitter.

That menacing front end is further enhanced by a contrasting matte black hood made of unpainted carbon fiber that has a huge power dome, raised to accommodate the Ford Racing 5.0-liter 440-horsepower V-8 that is nestled in the engine bay.

The fenders are made more muscular with flared wheel arches to accommodate the wider racing slicks, and large air extractors—one positioned high on the front fender just ahead of the door and another low behind the rear wheel—add additional detailing to the sides. Chromed

*Also influencing the design of the GT-R was the 1970 Mustang Mach 1, particularly in the area of the split headlamp treatment.*

*The Mustang GT-R sits lower to the ground, hunkered down over 20-inch Pirelli racing slicks.*

exhaust tips exit just ahead of the rear wheels. The C-pillar windows are blanked-out with another air extractor on the right side, while the left one is fitted with the filler neck for the fuel cell.

Five-spoke 20-inch alloy wheels have been cut from billet and are shod with P275/35/20 front and P315/30/20 rear Pirelli slicks. The wide-open spokes reveal Brembo brakes with six-piston front and four-piston rear calipers gripping 14.3-inch front and 13.0-inch rear rotors.

The rear of the GT-R is fitted with a huge carbon fiber wing and a lower rear carbon fiber diffuser.

A honeycomb grille covering the cooler for the rear differential divides the signature three-element taillamps.

Inside, the GT-R is a work of racing art. A single Sparco racing seat dominates the spartan body-colored interior. The doors, which still open conventionally and reaffirm the GT-R's status as a "door-slammer," are fitted with carbon fiber panels that blend into the carbon fiber dash. The vents and speedometer and tachometer bezels are covered over by carbon fiber. The only two conventional gauges are the oil temperature and ammeter, which flank a large kill switch in the center of

*The purposeful look of the GT-R concept is enhanced by the huge rear wing and carbon fiber diffuser attached beneath the rear fascia.*

the dash. Beneath that switch is a row of secondary toggle switches to control the lights and cooling fans. The GT-R is fitted with a Formula One–style steering wheel with digital readouts for vehicle speed, engine revs, and other functions, while a row of lights aids the driver in shifting at the 7,000 rpm redline.

"Most racers cobble together interiors," Gaffka explains. "The Formula One–style wheel significantly reduces dash gauges to help preserve Mustang's powerful instrument panel." This also contributes to a clean, purposeful look of the interior that echoes the exterior design.

The steering wheel, however, is the only modern touch; there's no paddle shift or other high-tech bits to the interior. The gearbox has a large slap shifter, while the pedals are machined out of aluminum. The rear seat area is fitted with a fire-suppression system.

It's a pure race car in the sense of the original Trans-Am, which featured modified production cars, as opposed to the purpose-built plastic-bodied tube frame racers found in that series today.

Structurally, the GT-R utilizes a stock Mustang steel unit body into which a roll cage was welded. The concept retains 85 percent of the production car's body parts.

*While the basic shape is all Mustang, the nose of the GT-R is much more aggressive, with a widely spaced honeycomb pattern on the larger grille, a bigger lower intake, front splitter, and projector-beam headlamps.*

*The bold GT-R graphics sit above a large air extractor positioned right behind the front wheels. Six-piston Brembo calipers can be seen behind the five-spoke alloy wheels.*

The only modifications were the rear-mounted batteries and the fuel cell installed in the trunk area. The car retains its production suspension geometry, although many of its components are made of lightweight chrome-moly pieces. The rear also remains a solid rear axle with three links, although the shocks have been replaced with coil-over fully adjustable units with remote reservoirs. In addition, the 1.25-inch Panhard rod and anti-sway bar are race-spec components.

Beneath the hood is a 5.0-liter (302-ci) dual overhead cam Ford Racing crate engine making 440 horsepower at 7,000 rpm and 400 ft-lb of torque at 5,500 rpm. The four-valve aluminum engine has an 11:1 compression ratio, ported heads, higher-lift cams,

*More show than go, the exhaust tips have been chromed to call attention to the fact that they exit the side of the vehicle.*

high-flow fuel injectors, and a magnesium variable-geometry intake manifold. The exhaust system includes custom Tri-Y headers that feed into crossover side exhausts. Called the "Cammer," this V-8 has been tuned to produce more than 550 horsepower in GrandAm's Daytona Prototype class.

The engine is mated to a Tremec T56 six-speed manual transmission via a heavy-duty racing clutch and flywheel assembly taken from the Mustang Cobra R. The driveshaft is made from a metal-alloy composite and feeds into a Winters/Ford 9-inch rear differential with a 4.56:1 final drive ratio.

According to Dan Davis, who heads up Ford Racing, the GT-R shows what could be done with the 2005 Mustang using off-the-shelf components from Ford's performance parts catalog. Retailing for $14,995, the Cammer engine, combined with the other components shown on the GT-R, would put a full-race Mustang in the $40,000 to $50,000 range, much more affordable than many of the stock-based cars racing.

"The GT-R is the Mustang racers would build if they weren't bound by various road racing rules," Davis notes.

"The Mustang GT-R could be adapted to conform to different series and budgets, but in this variation, serves as a dream machine."

That dream would be a return to the legendary Trans-Am battles of the late 1960s and early 1970s in which the factories went door-to-door in cars that were far more stock than modified. Ford hopes the GT-R sparks some interest in the racing community for a shift back to this type of racing, although company officials are keenly interested in stepping up the Mustang's road racing presence by modifying the concept to comply with rules in such series as the American LeMans, SCCA Trans-Am, GrandAm Cup, and FIA GT racing. The Mustang GT-R could also form the basis of a turnkey grassroots package offered by Ford Racing.

## THE MANY FACES OF MUSTANG

The different front-end treatment of the Mustang GT-R, which is similar to one of the designs for the production car that made it to the clay stage, indicates that while the basic body shape of the current car is set, there will be a whole host of newer models that play off different themes.

*Behind the rear wheel, another vent allows air to escape the underbody, an aid in cooling the brakes.*

*The quarter window on the driver's side has been covered over and provides the fill-point for the trunk-mounted fuel cell.*

*The passenger-side quarter window has been covered over with a scoop that recalls Shelby Mustangs.*

J Mays says all his research into the Mustang history demonstrated that there are many different looks the car can have and still be true to the nameplate.

"There is no one front end to the Mustang," Mays explains. "Some had the headlamps inboard, some had the headlamps outboard, some had the fog lamps low, some had no fog lamps. The Mustang logo can be in the middle of the grille or over to the left. There will be different grille textures. All of these become visual cues that allow us to play different flavors with the car. So right now we have the V-6 and the GT and eventually we get the SVT Cobra and there will be other variations that

The carbon fiber hood is unpainted, giving it a matte black appearance from a distance. The power dome provides additional clearance under the hood for the Cammer engine.

Below: *This 5.0-liter dual overhead cam V-8 came straight from the Ford Performance Racing catalog and produces 440 horsepower and 400 ft-lb of torque. A specially modified intake system helps boost the engine's output.*

people have alluded to. But our inspirations for these special models have been the Bullitt, the GT350, the GT500, the Boss, the Mach 1, the 428s and 429s."

Both the Bullitt and Mach 1 were bona fide hits in the last generation Mustang, so both models will likely see a return engagement at some point in time. Many of these new models were positioned for launches after the

first two years or so of regular Mustang production. The plan was to roll out special models slowly as demand for the V-6 and GT models was met and sales began to soften. The sequencing for the Mustang launch had coupes first, followed by convertibles, and then the SVT Mustang Cobra. Beyond that, look for models like the Bullitt, Mach 1, Boss 302, etc., in limited model runs of

fun. Somewhere along the line, we might even create a couple of regional Mustangs."

Primarily the areas that will be changed on future models, as the GT-R demonstrates, will be the front fascia, hood, and side details that can be altered by add-on rocker panels and fender extensions. Most of these items are soft trim that is relatively low cost and easy to tool, as opposed to changing stamped body panels.

Other areas that can be easily changed include the quarter window treatments, which can be blanked out as on the GT-R or louvered, and the rear end, which can be fitted with any number of wings and spoilers from mild to wild. And the flexibility of the interior provides room to apply different materials, sew patterns, and trim pieces that fit in with the overall design of the special package.

The important thing to Mays, however, is that the car's basic proportion and surfacing remain the same, that there is some constancy in the Mustang heritage. "One of the things I want to do with the car is to let all the customers know that they're buying something that is not going off in a completely different direction next week."

In other words, the desire to reinvent the Mustang and replace it with a front-drive car like the Probe is dead. But that doesn't mean the Mustang will always come in one flavor. Mays said there are at least 50 variations to the front end that could be done and still be all Mustang.

*If history is any indication of what sort of future special-edition Mustangs may be in the pipeline, the smart money is on a modern interpretation of the Boss series.*

5,000 units or so. Mays believes there's even more opportunity for additional limited-production models based on geography.

"We've even dug so deep into the archives, we've discovered there was a Mustang sold for a short period of time in Colorado called the High Country," Mays says. "It had all these kinds of little tricks on them and they're just

*Since the Mustang GT-R incorporates some design themes seen on earlier Mustang clay models, it's possible that many of these styling elements will appear on future variants.*

*In the future, as this sketch illustrates, the Mustang could take a more modern and aggressive tack with sharper character lines, a larger front grille, a different hood, and a bigger rear wing.*

Then there's the aftermarket. The Mustang has long been a favorite of tuners like Roush, Saleen, and Kenny Brown. The new design, greater base horsepower, and improved suspension give these quasi-factory tuners a new blank canvas to create their own interpretations of this American classic. With the first all-new platform in 25 years, there no doubt will be a new Mustang revolution in showrooms and the aftermarket.

"One thing I think about a lot is how people are going to react to the new Mustang over the long haul," Mays says. "I'm hoping it's very positive." The ability to change and adapt the Mustang to not only rekindle fond memories of the old car, but also to create new versions that will appeal to younger buyers with no sense of that history, is critical to long-term success.

That doesn't mean the 2005 Mustang's design is fixed for all time. Already Mays and his designers are looking much farther down the road, at the next generation car.

"With this design, I consider we got the car back on track," Mays says. "As with any of these cars that have heritage tied to them, I feel we have gone and put the car back to the way it was intended to evolve. Now we can move forward. I'm very keen on doing a modern one next time around."

*The interior is bare bones, just like a race car. A large slapstick shifter for the six-speed manual projects from the center tunnel, while the Formula One-inspired steering wheel, with its digital readout, almost seems out of place. The dash and parts of the door are covered in carbon fiber.*

# Index